PHENOMENAL, THAT'S ME!

PHENOMENAL, THAT'S ME!

(STILL STANDING)

Contributing Authors

Tra-C J. Pierce
Evangelist Patsy Cross-Cole
Mia Turner-Whitley
Joyce Petry Montgomery
Dr. Sarah Ransom
Kendra Dee
Dianne "Pastor di" Matthews
Teresa Beene
Jennifer Nash
Kayla Roberts
Alida Smith
Kamekio Lewis

ISBN: 151682976X
ISBN-13: 9781516829767

FOREWORD

PHENOMENAL, THAT'S ME! Still Standing is a dynamic set of 12 stories from 12 women that have had a variety of experiences, all types of adversity; each victorious in their journeys tell their stories to empower, encourage, engaged women to find that Phenomenal Spirit that lives within them and walk in it!

Tra-C J. Pierce is the founder of a group call Phenomenal Women, Inc. It is Tra-C's desire to empower women to find their passion, their purpose, and pursue their place and stand in their position as a Phenomenal Women. Tra-C envisioned writing a book using different women with different stories that could collaborate, co-author, co-exist as one consortium and compile their stories to create a catalyst to reach women with diverse lifestyles and issues.

This book will encourage those that have battled sickness and disease, domestic violence, physical, mental and emotional abuse. It will help those that struggle with forgiveness, self-esteem, poverty, homelessness, the jobless, those that need faith, those grieving loss, such as death and divorce. It will strengthen those that have gone through depression, incarceration, family dysfunction, the welfare of their children and their walk with GOD.

This book is a tool to let women know that GOD made each of us Phenomenal and we have the right and the power to walk as phenomenal women through every situation and every circumstance. I believe that you will find this book encouraging, uplifting, motivating and impactful.

FOREWORD

I encourage you to step into each chapter with each woman and walk the path with them, see what they did, learn from their mistakes and gain much from their experiences. I believe you will enjoy this book and realize just how phenomenal you really are!

Pastor Dianne Matthews
Dallas, Texas

TABLE OF CONTENTS

Foreword · v

Acknowledgments· ix

Chapter 1   In Search of Purpose
             Tra-C J Pierce ·2

Chapter 2   Victory Beyond the Valley of Pain
             Evangelist Patsy Cross-Cole · · · · · · · · · · · · · · · 12

Chapter 3   Standing After Divorce
             Mia Turner-Whitley· · · · · · · · · · · · · · · · · · · ·22

Chapter 4   Walking Through the Shadows of Death
             Joyce Petry Montgomery · · · · · · · · · · · · · · · · ·32

Chapter 5   After All This, I Am Still Phenomenal
             Dr. Sarah Ransom· ·42

Chapter 6   Interruption of the Plan
             Kendra Dee ·52

Chapter 7   Phenomenal Woman! Me? Yes Me!
             Dianne "Pastor di" Matthews· · · · · · · · · · · · · · ·60

Chapter 8   The Turning Point
             Teresa Beene ·72

Chapter 9   Divinely Restored
             Jennifer Nash ·84

Chapter 10   Pain, Praise and Perseverance
             Kayla Roberts ·96

Chapter 11   Life Unexpected
             Alida Smith ·104

Chapter 12 Making Progress, Not Excuses
                Kamekio Lewis · 116
                About The Authors · 129

ACKNOWLEDGMENTS

We acknowledge our Heavenly Father; by Him all things are made possible. We thank Him for the courage to take such a giant, unimaginable leap of faith and allow us to share our stories.

We would like to acknowledge and thank all of our friends and family for their support. We thank each of you for your prayers and encouragement. It is our goal to touch your life in a phenomenal way as well as inspire you as you inspire others.

CHAPTER 1

IN SEARCH OF PURPOSE

Tra-C J Pierce

"Once you identify your passion, you will discover your purpose."

FRUSTRATED WITH THE hand that life dealt me; staring with tear-stained eyes wondering if my life would every amount to anything. I wondered if God would find my life to be worth His while. Convincing myself that He would because the life that I had was the one He gave me. Many times I would find myself in love with God and frustrated with Him at the same time. Not satisfied with just existing, I wanted more, so much more. I needed more. I need to touch lives and inspire people. I always felt that there was someone else living inside of me just screaming to get out and announce to the world that I existed. Many years I dealt with an identity crisis because I really didn't know who I was. I was surrounded by people who were secure on their jobs while I hopped from job to job. I witnessed people running successful businesses while I would start and stop businesses, sometimes in the same day. I was far from Phenomenal, right? Not necessarily, because you can be a phenomenal woman in the making which is exactly who I was. Allow me to open my heart to you and share the most pivotal point in my life.

My name is Tra-C J Pierce and I am a "Phenomenal Woman!" I was born in Houston, Texas to my parents, Nell Jones and Noble Lee Barrett. I was born right in the heart of 5th ward. We were a very poor family. We survived on food stamps and government cheese, which made the best grilled cheese sandwiches. Trust me; if your family was poor like mine, where the cheese came from would be the least of your worries. You were more concerned about when the next one would come. I am the youngest of 5 siblings and favored by my mother who recently passed away. There is no word to express how much I miss her. Her passing has to be one of the most difficult life instances that I have had to face. I realize that dying is a huge part of living.

When I was 6 yrs old, my mother discovered that I could sing. She would have me sing to her friends for entertainment and they would pay me $1. As I grew older I realized that my love for the stage and performing for people was very appealing to me. I began starring in plays and later dancing in theaters. While performing I knew there was something unique about me that was different from my siblings. At that time I didn't know what the difference was. I was far too young to know what God's purpose was for my life. I also didn't know that it would take many years until it would be discovered. As I continued to grow and experience life, I witnessed a lot of pain. Not only because we were a poor family but mostly because of bad decisions. Still I knew deep down inside my life would take a different turn. Traveling this particular road was the assignment and so I had no choice.

My school days were fun and exciting because of who I was. I made a name for myself, which will remain anonymous. I wasn't as astute as the next student, although I could have been. School really didn't hold my attention unless there was a talent show or something that allowed me to perform. The only thing that really held my attention was the stage. When I would ask to be excused to go to the restroom; it wasn't because nature called but rather my desire to be on the stage. I would use my bathroom break for a chance to sing in the halls.

Despite the many turns that my life took, I still knew that I was called to greatness, but at that time I thought I would be famous and very rich. I can't say that those desires have changed very much, but they have definitely been altered.

As I started getting older, my life started becoming more meaningful. My focus really shifted off myself and onto others. I realized that I had passion for other things rather than just the stage. I accepted Christ when I was about 18. I had fallen hopelessly in love and it resulted in broken heart. Accepting Christ was the greatest and smartest thing I could have done with my foolish and simple life. I truly believe that's when passion became so vivid and obvious to me. It's something about having Christ in my life; He gives meaning and purpose to life. That's what my life sincerely needed…purpose. I spent a lot of time at church learning about Christ and His mission, His character and His influence. There is a song that comes to mind that was recorded by the late, great James Cleveland. The song is called "I want to be ready." There is a part in the song that makes me tear up each time I hear it. "Make me and mold me into something worthwhile." Wow! I want my life to be worth something. I don't want to just exist, I want to live, live largely and live with purpose.

PASSION TO GIVE

As I continued on this road, I noticed along the way I started to develop passion. I developed passion for giving. I wanted to give my time, my money and any other resources that I was blessed with. I somehow felt that everything God had given me was for someone else, so I started giving. To me, if you don't have a passion for this, you could really be living a self-centered life. That has to be a boring way to live, because it means that you only have passion for yourself or the things that concern you.

PASSION TO SERVE

I developed passion to serve. I get extreme pleasure from serving others. So desperate to serve, I started serving in my neighborhood. There is an elderly couple who could not properly care for themselves. Periodically I would round up my neighbor and kids to go and help them. We would donate several hours to cleaning for them to bring order to their surroundings. There was something inside of me that wanted to minister to them and so I did. I decided that each day I was blessed to see, I would look for the opportunity to serve. If I saw someone that needed a ride, I would offer it. If someone were behind me at a fast food place, I would pay for their meal. If someone needed help with a bill, I would pay it. I was determined to serve someone, and it really didn't matter what it cost.

PASSION TO ACHIEVE

By convincing myself that God has called me to greatness, I wanted to achieve something extraordinary. I was invited to speak for a Pastor in Milwaukee, WI, to about 300 women. It was a moving experience that I will never forget. After it was over, several attendees asked if I had written or published anything. Needless to say, the light bulb came on. I immediately started writing. I published my first book in 2001 It was a complete disaster. I must admit there are a few good points in the book but over-all very poorly written, but that's ok, I have a lot to say so I continued to write. I write with the intent of getting better and better.

PASSION TO INSPIRE

I'm really not sure how I became a Motivational Speaker. I realized that I could deliver encouraging words in an extraordinary and provoking way. I was called into the ministry at the age of 23 shortly after I married. I never received any proper training for ministry, but still I knew that God had called me to this area of ministry, so I moved forward with it. I went from speaking to writing books to quoting or writing adages. I wrote my first quote in 2001. "Those who want to achieve greatness must be willing to be shaped by those who have." I think it's a great quote. Since then I have written many to the tune of about 200.

Inspiring people is a mission for me. I honestly feel that God put me here for that purpose. That's really all I want out of life is to inspire someone to live better, love better and just be better.

PASSION TO CHANGE

As I consider the words Phenomenal Woman, another characteristic comes to my mind, humility. Now, I haven't always demonstrated humility. In fact the truth be told, I was an ugly person because I was just the opposite. I didn't want to admit it, but someone who I know loves me brought it to my attention…that being my mom. I didn't like the things she said but they were said to help me and not to hurt me. We must learn to differentiate between constructive and destructive criticism. Humility is the character that Christ demonstrated constantly. I realized that if I wanted to be more like Christ, then I needed to make some changes. I wanted my character to be overhauled. I didn't like who I was. I think it's important to like yourself; after all you will have to live with yourself for a long time.

THE SEARCH

I committed to seeking the Lord trying to learn what my purpose was. I saw people all around me fulfilling their purpose while mine remained unbeknownst to me. There are no words to describe how frustrating, aggravating and upsetting this was for me. It seemed that God was just silent. I wondered if I was in His way or if I was trying too hard to discover it. I really didn't know what to think many times. Then I developed very low self-esteem, which led to depression. Depression, you inquire? Yes depression. You know it is possible for the believer to become depressed. I turned my back on the church because I thought it was a joke. I spent the majority of my days in my bathrobe crying. I am not sure why there were so many tears, maybe it was because God was silent and I felt useless. I am sure there are many people who could care less about things like purpose and passion. I am not that person to say the least. I wanted my life to have meaning.

For years I proceeded to chase God for answers. One thing that I was certain of if nothing else is that I knew I was blessed with a lot of whatever I had. I just needed to know what to do with it. I remember getting so frustrated, that I went upstairs to my guest room and refused to come out. I became very exhausted from living an ordinary life that had no purpose. Periodically, I would call one of the Co-authors Pastor Di and just cry out to her. I was so happy to know that God at least sent me to someone who really believed in me and knew that God had called me to greatness. She would encourage me with her thought provoking words. Everybody needs someone to believe in them. I'm not sure whether she became tired of my bellyaching but she remained faithful.

I thought I could find what I was looking for at church. That didn't happen as I anticipated. For years I watched others flourish, but I could not get a grip on how and what to do so that I could also flourish.

There were many people that would say to me, "One day God is going to use you in a mighty way despite what these people think," I would respond by saying, "thank you so much." In my mind, I would think, yeah right!

There were many days that I convinced myself to just given up on trying to lead an extraordinary life. It would only work for that moment. Shortly, I would strike out on the beaten path again in search of purpose. Many days I would look in the mirror and say to myself, "You are an extraordinary person, now go get it! Go get what? How? Where would these passionate words come from? More importantly who gave me the right to tell myself these words? Well the only thing I can conclude is the life-giver Himself. Despite me not knowing what and how I would achieve greatness; I still declared that it would be so. One day I would lead a purpose driven life and that HE has called me to greatness, really?

FROM PASSION TO PURPOSE

The search for purpose has not been an easy journey. It required patience, persistence and an undeniable will.

Pursuing my passion helped me to discover my purpose. Finding my purpose offered me an amazing rebirth experience that I will never forget; which is similar to an erupting volcano. As we know an erupting volcano has the powerful ability to do great damage, which was my mission. My mission was to destroy the idea that I had no purpose. It was for the purpose of destroying all seeds of doubt planted in my mind that God would ever use me. It also destroyed my lack of faith to believe that He called me to greatness.

The search for purpose also helped me to discover my reason for living. It helped me overcome numerous obstacles, weather many storms; accept abandonment and the refusal of defeat despite popular belief.

Anyone can live, but it takes courage to live with purpose. That's exactly how I live each day, with the intent to touch lives, be a bright spot, and demonstrate Christ-like character. These are my reasons for living. There are truly no words to describe this liberated sense of freedom that I have. For years I was living in prison. I was trapped and snared by the enemy who spoke lies in my ears daily. I dealt with the fear of abandonment. My siblings had abandoned me, which was difficult. The idea of being abandoned by God was unfathomable. Many days I would stare in the heavens pleading with God, "Don't leave me like this, don't leave me without purpose!" I had to fight to overcome, fight to survive and fight to achieve this victory.

Now, it's your turn. Are you in search of purpose? Are you tired of living an ordinary life? Have you convinced yourself that God has called you to greatness? I want to encourage you to discover your passion. What is it that you love doing whether you are paid to do it or not. Can you do this for the rest of your life? You might be surprised to know that your passion is mysteriously linked to your purpose. My purpose was very close to me, but I couldn't see it because I was looking too hard for it. When I thought God was silent, He was speaking all along. God moves in mysterious way, His wonders to perform. He may not speak to you as you expect or when you expect. There is one thing for sure-He is a faithful God. Rest assured that if He spoke it, He will perform it. He is God and He keeps His word a 1000 generations.

Let me leave you with this one thought. I want you to meditate on it day and night. I want you say it daily until you have convinced yourself of its truth. Jeremiah 29:11, "I know the plans I have for you declares the Lord. Plans to prosper you and not to harm you, plans to give you hope and a future." Don't let this scripture frustrate you because He knows the plans for your life and you don't. Let it give you hope and bring you peace. Allow it to guide you across the angry shores of life. Rest in it.

I am no longer sitting, staring and wondering. Now I am doing. I am doing exactly what He called me to do. I am serving His people, touching lives and influencing change. I am using the gifts that He gave me to change the world one person at a time. I am so honored and privileged to be recognized as a Phenomenal Woman. It actually holds me to a higher standard of living. I realize that is a huge title and not every woman can courageously wear it. I have had my share of pain, struggles, flaws and failure, but I am still standing and I am still in the fight and that is what makes me Phenomenal.

C H A P T E R   2

VICTORY BEYOND THE VALLEY OF PAIN

Evangelist Patsy Cross-Cole

"Breathe in life...Embrace the moment...Cherish the journey."

I INVITE YOU to walk with me into this time capsule where images of my past come to life right before your eyes.

As a bushy-haired little girl, living in a country town in Texas, where the sounds of crickets echoed, I had already possessed some of the character traits of a "Phenomenal Woman". I had a rousing spirit, a joyful soul; I believe my father and mother thought I was amazing. Most of the teachers all rated me as being exceptional. The preacher sometimes viewed me as being extraordinary, and my friends treated me like I was fantastic. Sounds phenomenal right?

And then…it was as if my picture-perfect life as a young girl immediately transformed into a scene out of a horror movie. The shock of what was happening to me sent triggers throughout my mind. In one single thought, I shouted out from the depth of my soul a series of questions: "who, what, when, where, how and why"? My childhood imagination was suddenly interrupted by the disturbances of the moment. The swing stopped swinging; the merry-go round quit revolving, the chanting of nursery rhymes became faint and the clown's face was no longer funny. Without notifications or warnings, no time to pack, prepare or pray, I was relocated to the "Valley of Pain".

I was frozen with fear and intimidation. There I lay helpless, hopeless and wide-eyed, watching the thief rob me of my innocence. Sometime around 1972, at the young age of 12, I had become a victim of identity theft. I knew in every fiber of my being I would never be the same. I could not be the same! Psychologically, nothing made sense. It wasn't that I was naïve to this type of act taking place, even in our small peaceful town, but I knew him! He knew me! We were very well acquainted!

We were…! It was all over so quickly. In the midst of the pain, shame and disgust, time seemed to have stood still. For some reason, those short moments felt like a century. My head was pounding and I was literally sick to my stomach. It was as if the pain had suctioned my total being into a vacuum with no way of escape.

There were days when 24 hours was just too much. As those long days and sleepless nights passed, I wanted so much to reveal the details of what felt like a "Death Valley" experience. Was it fear that held my mouth shut tight? Due to the familiarity, I knew I was not afraid of him. However, I believe it was the circumstances that surrounded me that contributed to my fear. The questions that I constantly rehearsed in my mind were, "What about my family? What will be their response to this information?"

I had a warm childhood while being raised alongside 7 siblings. I perceived my parents to be the best a child could dream of having. They were both skillful with great qualities. It is the strength of my mom in my genes that enabled me to write this story. I lived in a home where good morals, manners and Christian values were taught. Our small community was like having one big happy family. Parents held true to the belief that, "It takes a village to raise a child". Everyone was accountable to each other. I could not imagine exposing the truth at the expense of being labeled as a "fast-tailed" little girl or even a "lying" little girl. In both cases my reputation would be destroyed and my experience of being "phenomenal" would soon cease.

The feelings of guilt, embarrassment and shame, dominated the thoughts of this innocent 12-year-old girl. Apparently over a period of time, that same thief invaded my mind and began convincing me that maybe that incidence was my fault. Questions such as, "Was I really innocent? Was it possible that I did something to encourage this type of behavior? If I decided to break the silence, could I be viewed as an accomplice in this criminal act?"

I continued to bombard my mind and overwhelm myself with question after question. I even rationalized as to whether or not it was really considered molestation. After all, there was indeed an established relationship with the perpetrator. Yet, never in my worst nightmare would I have envisioned a pure relationship resulting into something so filthy and detestable.

The sexual abuse continued over a period of two years. Every time I saw him he seemed to be acting normal, while I would have given anything to have some type of normalcy in my life. Of course, I was still able to maintain my friendships, achieve academic excellence, conduct my household chores and perform during my high school basketball games. But when all the noise in my life came to a screeching halt, lurking in the corridors of my mind were those tormenting spirits. That's exactly who they were! Their assignment was to persuade me to remain silent and embrace this "Death Valley" journey as my permanent destination. I must admit at the time they were successful. I began to think no one would ever believe me and that the consequences of telling someone would be far worse than the wrongful act itself. Therefore, like many others before me, and those that would visit this valley after me, I chose to suffer in silence…never a word uttered to anyone.

While in the Valley of Pain, the enemy has an agenda to disarm every ounce of your faith, disturb your peace and break your spirit. Although during the last few years of high school, I never displayed any signs of depression, the reality of being molested consumed my mind, lowered my self-esteem and crippled my efforts of ever demonstrating sexual purity. No! I didn't lose my virginity-It was stolen! I found myself challenged with fornication and losing the battle. Sadly, I would never be granted the blessed opportunity of celibacy prior to marriage. I would one day stand before a clergyman, looking into the eyes of my future husband having a distorted view of sex. As a young Christian, I sometimes asked how God could allow this to happen to me. I was being punished for sure. Yet, deep down in my heart underneath the lies of the enemy, there was that still small voice of truth. I knew this just wasn't fair and I did nothing to deserve it!

Traveling through this valley was like being in a den of hungry lions, hoping to come out alive. The molestation and then the trauma of feeling violated haunted me for years. The evil seeds planted beyond that day robbed me of self-worth. I felt my value had been determined by someone else, someone who sent me the message that my body was not my own and my choices were meaningless. My thought process and inner core were deeply damaged.

As a highly motivated college student, the struggle to find my identity was real. Never asking the Holy Spirit to guide me, I searched in drugs, social organizations, and nightlife entertainment. I found myself entangled in relationships that God did not ordain. I often indulged in overeating and drowned myself in alcohol hoping to dull my senses of reality and numb my pain. This image was far from my childhood reflection of a "Phenomenal Woman." The memories were painstaking! I tried to sleep them away, drink them away, smoke them away or just ignore them away!

The unavoidable effects of pain have the tendency to deplete every positive thought in your mind. Finally, as a young adult, the depression began to overshadow me; suicidal thoughts reached out to grab me, and I felt like I was being engulfed in flames. So much pain! The walls of despair were closing in on me. I even found myself terrified to sleep alone at night while having reoccurring nightmares.

My valley experience was definitely a place of uncertainties. I had no idea the direction my future was headed. The worldly pleasures and my sinful exploits had erected a bridge between God and me. I no longer felt His presence but I seriously needed Him. I knew the right choices for me, but lacked the strength and stamina to act upon them. In desperation, I began offering "panting prayers," whispering, "God please help me! I cannot endure this pain! Please rescue me from this valley!"

At the time I did not realize it was God that had place signs in the valley labeled "Stop", "Detour", "Dead End", and "Do Not Enter". However, choosing to be led by my emotions, I had ignored them all. I entered a "Danger Zone" and became a single mom during my senior year in college. The light said to be at the end of the tunnel is designed to give you hope. For some reason, it only made me aware of how deep in darkness I really was.

Although I remained in the valley, the many responsibilities that came with motherhood thrust me into the arms of the one who promised to "never leave nor forsake me". The cry of my soul was to be set free. It was then when I discovered that the valley is not always quiet.

In my distress, I could hear God telling me to "cast all my cares on him, because he cared for me". It was such a breath of fresh air and comfort to know that even in my disobedience, He was willing to speak to me.

During my last semester, I realized I was not alone; grace and mercy had followed me throughout my entire college career. Those faint prayers offered to God had been heard after all. Some of my most challenging years, He had saved me from self-destruction over and over again. I had been granted the discipline and determination required to focus on my education endeavors. As a result, I qualified to be placed on the Academic Deans List three consecutive semesters. I recall my parents being so proud, which was always important to me even as a child.

Pain has the potential to restrict or restrain you from reaching future goals. The box of fear from my past had confined me for too long. I knew that an attempt to chart my own course and determine my own destiny would ultimately lead to my ruin. After coming face to face with that truth, I resumed to my daily Bible reading. The word of God gave me such a burst of inspiration. He showed me how to see Him even when it was dark.

Many years, the words echoed in my mind, "weeping may endure for a night, but joy comes in the morning". Morning seems so far away when you're in the valley. Daylight appears to be held hostage prolonging the misery and pain. God revealed to me the damage that had taken my joy.

The abuser had squeezed me in such a tight grip that almost choked the life out of me. As I continued to lean and depend on God, my breathing was regulated and life began to have a brand new meaning. Later, against all odds, I became a member of Who's Who among Students of Colleges and Universities and earned a Bachelor of Science Degree.

Every pain experienced is a type of pilgrimage; it's leading you to a nearby destination or to a faraway distance. Somehow I knew I was surrounded by mountains and on the other side of either mountain was a straight and narrow path. I yearned to reach that path. I wanted to move forward pass my painful experiences but I just had trouble taking my foot off the brakes. All along while setting up a tent in the valley, I envisioned my life being fruitful and productive.

For years I had missed out on the freedom of giving love and receiving love. I resented men's authority because of the pain I endured at the hand of a man. The truth is pain changes its shape over hours, weeks, months and years. God's sustaining power and my obedience toward Him allowed me to make my exit from that dark, dry place. Finally, I decided to take baby steps toward victory by trusting a man with my heart. Though still slightly bruised, I was willing to give it away and did just that. I spent the next years of my life fulfilling the role as a wife, mother and laborer, while serving weekly in the local church.

Life and its fierce winds continued to blow. Among the common challenges young married couples encountered, we were experiencing great financial hardships. At that time, I was the mother of two with the youngest being one year old. The three words I was shocked to hear were, "you are pregnant". Yes! This caught us by surprise. Obviously, we didn't attend Planned Parenthood classes and having another baby at this stage was not on our agenda. That quiet still voice, which led me through the valley, was willing to guide me through this. I knew in my spirit I needed to stand still and see the salvation of the Lord. However, after much thought, but little prayer, the conclusion was to have an abortion.

Our decision made sense and seemed necessary in order to maintain the household obligations, but it did not make FAITH. My Christian values and motherly instincts were in opposition of this decision. Unfortunately, to remain silent when suffering had been woven in the fibers of my soul. Therefore, I never shared my true feelings about the plans to commit to the abortion process. Seeking counsel or the opinion of others never entered my mind. There was no question that my reputation as a strong Christian woman was about to be compromised. Nevertheless, without any coercion, I decided to follow through with the decision.

How does one set an appointment to kill an innocent human being? I arrived at the clinic early that morning. The big day was here; not to bring forth a life but to take a life. The abortion preparation that was packaged with lies seemed like eternity. I'm sure there was some correlation between Hell and this place. It seemed so familiar although I had never been there. All of the medical staff was in uniform. (*Evil always comes dressed up in a costume.*) The interior had beautiful pictures; the walls were freshly painted with colors intended to relax you. I was everything *but* relaxed.

As I laid face down on that cold table, I was tossed to and fro in my faith and beliefs. God was unveiling my eyes to see the truth regarding my decision. He informed me that the seed I had carried in my womb for 5 months was more than tissue and blood; rather he was a human being with a divine purpose. Sounding like a Commanding Officer to his soldier in the time of war, the Holy Spirit instructed me to get dressed, reverse the American Express charges and walk out the door. I immediately understood why this place seemed familiar. The same evil force I yielded to during my "Death Valley" experience was in this clinic. The anesthesia was having strong effects on my body, but I was influenced more by the words I was hearing in my spirit.

The next few minutes of my life mimicked moments in the Matrix. Although I was moving slow, I was moving with power! I developed a warrior mentality and dared anyone to get in my way! I wasn't physically blind, but there was an activation of tunnel vision taking place. Determined to follow God's instruction, I was focused and went straight toward the counter window and reversed the charges. With no explanation given, we walked right out that door.

I felt like a champion that day. There was a battle that took place in my mind between good and evil, but thanks to God, I overcame evil with good. I didn't just save a seed…I didn't just save my child…I saved a life! We had no regrets beyond that day to the present concerning the final decision. Four months later, we became the proud parents of a handsome baby boy! Years later, I wondered whether I possessed that same power to save my marriage. The struggles and challenges had increased rapidly. Certain situations with our relationship prompted me to prepare myself for another trip to the valley. I had no desire to visit that place ever again.

This time after 10 years of marriage, divorce was the ticket that took me back to the valley. Shortly after my divorce, I found myself on an emotional rollercoaster. I was tempted to demonstrate the same destructive behavior that never brought me comfort. God had granted me so much grace over the years. Therefore, I refused to repeat my past addictive attachments. I had a choice to become immobilized by my crisis or rise from the pain and embrace the most precious gift from God… life itself. I chose the latter.

After becoming a single parent of four wonderful children, I was in need of energy for the great journey ahead. I needed a hiding place to recoup from the noise of my trials…a place of peace…a place of refuge and rest. God is so faithful! Interestingly, He provided an escape route in the valley where I was able to hide under the shadow of His wings. I was still broken from the divorce, but in my pain, I stumbled upon strength. It was there that I was renewed, rejuvenated and refreshed.

As the years passed, still walking through deserts and valleys, I totally surrendered my life to serving God, and then He sent a wonderful loving man cross my path who I later married. While growing in Godly wisdom, I realized that life would always consist of valleys, mountains and plateaus. I was very familiar with valleys and plateaus. I even witnessed God's hand of deliverance while in the valley. I was ready now to experience something new, *"victory beyond the valley of pain"*. Sadly, there was one thing hindering me from doing so.

One Sunday, during my time of worship, God showed me the ugly root of bitterness in my heart caused by un-forgiveness. I'll never forget the day I stood before a church congregation and made a confession that I had been victimized as a child. That was one of the hardest things I had ever done, but the deliverance that followed was liberating. Every day I had spent in the valley of pain was designed to bring me to a place…that place being one of complete trust in God. I stood there at the altar taking my pain off life support and giving it to Him. I was willing to undergo surgery of the heart in order to release me from the yoke of bondage.

There are times when it's hard to forgive maybe because we do not feel those who have hurt us deserve forgiveness. I learned that forgiveness is not a feeling it's a choice. A heavy burden was lifted when I chose to forgive my abuser and then led to forgive myself. I had taken that pain of my past around like a suitcase of merchandise for 36 years. Healing and wholeness was a byproduct of what took place on that day. I learned the bottom line of every painful experience in order to obtain victory is faith, and there is "*victory beyond the valley of pain.*"

I am a living witness of the power of God's word! He transformed my life by renewing my mind. As a Minister of the Gospel, I have a mandate to tell others of His saving grace and His mercy that endures forever. If you are *wounded, brokenhearted* or *hopeless,* the Good News is *Victory* can be yours today!

Every person has a story, but not all stories are shared. My only intention in sharing mine is to lead someone to victory that find themselves held captive while traveling through the valley of pain.

I give Glory to God for giving me the courage needed to share my tragedies and triumphs through the tool of writing. In doing so, I have become inspired to continue fulfilling my passion as an Author. I also express my appreciation to my husband, Mr. Cole and my children: Quincy, Charletra, Johnny, Joshua and Joshuwan. It is because of my love for them all that I endured the trials, fought the fight of faith and NEVER gave up!

Yes, it is true…Life has hit me with a few hard blows causing me to stagger at times…but through it all I can say, "I'm Still Standing."

CHAPTER 3

STANDING AFTER DIVORCE

Mia Turner-Whitley

"I've learned that people will forget what you said,
people will forget what you did, but people will never
forget how you made them feel."

MAYA ANGELOU

I WAS so numb. Mentally, physically and spiritually I was a lifeless body. My life had turned upside down. I had so many questions without answers. I felt worse than a motherless child. I felt abandoned, beyond embarrassed and questioned who I was, my future, my well-being. I thought my marriage would be able to stand any test! I felt that we had such an awesome ministry together and that we would be going places spiritually. I looked forward to one day being a First Lady. I looked forward to the tent revivals and witnessing, bringing in souls for the kingdom. I was his biggest fan. No one could tell me anything about this man of God of mine! We worshipped and praised the Lord together, both in our home and in the church! People looked up to us and not a one of them along with me would have ever dreamt we would get a divorce. After all we loved the Lord and worshipped him in spirit and in truth. I thought I was the ideal wife and mother. Submissive was I. My children rose up and called me blessed; my husband was known and I brought him no shame.

One day in 1999 after 9 years of marriage some things started to change and before long had spiraled out of control. On October 2003 it ended at the Tarrant County Court House when the judge granted the divorce and told us to have a good life. That moment I felt free, but only for that moment. I didn't know what this new life would be like. A part of me was relieved; most of me was in so much pain. After all I had to let go all the dreams we had and turn them to my dreams. I had to feel my way through this big old world by myself without him. My parents who lived in Illinois wanted me to come back home, but I loved Texas and I was not about to let divorce run me away. So, I stayed here in pain and agony. The word of God was yet in my heart. I knew God was there and he was providing for me and my children, yet at times I felt so alone and distant from him. I never blamed God for what I was going through. Many times in my prayer closet I cried out to the Lord Why me? Why us? Many days I was disobedient to the word of God by being rebellious, stubborn and in denial. Psalms 40:2 says, "He brought me up also out of an horrible pit, out of the miry clay, and set my feet upon a rock, and established my goings." I cannot tell you how many times I found myself in the mire. I was stuck and could not move forward. I was moving backwards. When I would to do good, evil was always present and sometimes I found myself in sin time and time again. I was in places that I knew I had no business, or I was saying or doing things I knew I should have not. This appeared to be my new normal and when I finished grieving I knew I had to get up, stand up and keeping moving. I can't tell you how many times I fell down to my knees, or flat on my face. In spite of all those emotions on this emotional rollercoaster, I had to keep moving, one step at a time and one day at a time. I had to smile as though I was still on top of the world, because after all people were watching, people were wondering, how can she be so strong? How can she still smile? How can she keep moving on? I had my children. They needed me. I felt I was all they had and if I couldn't keep moving for me, at least do it for them.

I truly feel that I had a functional mental breakdown. I had to get up and go to work to pay the bills and keep food on the table. Each day I would come home and make sure my children ate, did their chores and schoolwork, I would go in my room and lie in the bed and watch the television show Martin. Not laughing, just watching. I was so broken and depressed. How could I go from sitting behind my ex, a minister and the Bishop's adjutant to the back part of the church full of pain, animosity and hopelessness? I am not writing these things to have anyone feel sorry for me, but to realize that Divorce is not as easy as it seems. It's so much better to work it out if possible. If for whatever reason that is not possible, then get ready for one of the worse battles of one's life, but it definitely does not have to be the end. Going through the ups and downs broke me down, but yet I still had to wear this mask called a smile. I am a private person and I had a very small circle that I would confide in, but do you really tell one person everything? They say divorce is worse than death; I like to add it's probably because if you have children with them you still have to communicate with them on some level. At that point in my life I didn't want to, and when I did it was because I had to for my kid's sake. We were all lost. My two younger children (elementary age) were too young to understand, or realize what was happening. My teenagers were old enough and were exposed to our ugly reality. I felt for them because being a teenager alone was a trial and now dealing with our adult issues was a lot. Yet here I was a single parent again, only this time my baggage was heavier.

It's so easy to say, give it to God! Prayer changes things! He won't put more on you than you can bear! Your latter days will be greater than your former! All those uplifting and encouraging words are wonderful until you are going through a test! In order to get through it you have to go through it. There is no microwave process! Baking at 350 degrees for 35 minutes is what we have to do in order to fully come out done. This in turn means that healing from a broken heart and divorce takes time and is a process. The time can vary depending on the person. For me it took about 8 years to totally heal and be ready for a healthy relationship. I had to enter this next phase of my life being brutally honest with myself. My own truths, my own fears and my own realities were at the forefront of this chapter. I had to learn who Mia was and what is it that Mia wanted and expected out of her life. This was not an easy task because after self- inspection I realized that I had lost me in my marriage. I have learned in a healthy marriage no one loses themselves in the marriage, to the point that everything revolves around the wants, needs and desires of one person. We are in it together.

So here I was, in the valley of decision. Before we actually divorced we were living like roommates. We had a two story home and he moved me upstairs and he was in the master bedroom downstairs. February of 2003, my ex presented me with the divorce papers. According to the paper work we had to wait 3 months before we could go to the court to get officially divorced. During this time I was unemployed and attending school full time. In May of 2003, I earned my Bachelors in Psychology and Education. On Good Friday in 2003, my children and I were in a terrible accident and totaled my car, however God blessed and we all survived. I also learned that in October of 2003 I would be having my first grandchild. It was just so much. Finally, we were set to go to court in October of 2003; two days after the Lord blessed me with a new job and a week after the birth of my grandchild. I was full of so much anxiety and stress, but life continued on. Through my emotional and spiritual roller coasters I was experiencing earlier in this chapter, I found time to plan at least my next steps. Through it all somewhere within me I knew that my test were working to make me a better me. I did not quite understand everything, but I knew two things 1) someone was praying for me and that 2) one day I would be married again. Now initially I did go through the, "I will never get married again!" phase. Like most human beings, when we are experiencing something painful (for example, childbirth), we adamantly declare we will never do whatever caused the pain again.

Being in a relationship was the furthest thing from my mind. In fact, I was grieving. There are five stages in grieving: denial, anger, bargaining, depression and finally acceptance. At any time I would be floating between anger and depression because of the results of my marriage. So in between the arguments of where was I going to move, because against my will we were selling our home. This in and of itself was another whole mentally draining issue. It had been time for me to start my next move. This part of the journey was just as challenging. Now I would have to, on my own find a place for me and my four children to live. As I reflect back on that time, God was still our provider. He still put the right people in my path to help me. My beautician recommended a real estate agent who was helping us to sell our home, as well as help me find a new home for me and the children. He also offered to waive his fee, if we decided to take our house off the market before our contract was up.

In February of 2004, I finally moved into my own place. It was such an emotional moment. The steps you have to go through to rent a home was very stressful considering my credit was not the greatest. My realtor had me to write a letter explaining my situation and attach it to the application with lots of prayer and faith. God blessed us and it was the first place I moved to on my own in my own name. I remember one night I was feeling lonely and sad from just all that was transpiring in my life and I cried and cried and cried. Afterwards I made a promise to myself that I would not cry like that for those reasons ever again. What happened simply happened and it was time to continue to move on. I began to think about me for a change. What was it that I wanted for me for a change? What were my likes and dislikes? What does my voice sound like? Slowly I begin to really focus on me and what I wanted to do with my life.

Before I could fully start this journey I had to do something very critical and necessary. The first step I had to make was to forgive. Forgive myself, my ex-husband and anyone who was involved in us getting a divorce. I made up in my mind that I had to forgive myself in order to move towards my healing, and no longer have bitter feelings. I knew I needed to free myself, because holding on to the past and who harmed me was not going to allow me to successfully move to my future in a healthy manner. So I forgave us all for all that happened and what we did to one another. Once I forgave, I felt some relief. I started to move forward in introducing myself to me again. I married when I was 22 and I divorced when I was 35. This was a whole lot of getting to know me time to make up for. I did a lot of new and first things for me during that time. I changed my church membership for a year in an effort to find a new beginning in church homes. It was just a temporary moment. In fact, when the pastor opened the doors to the church when my children and I joined, he offered it to be a temporary place unless the Lord leads you to permanently join. That meant a lot to me because I didn't know how long I would actually be there. For that moment it was a blessing. I was strengthened by the word and became stronger in that short amount of time. During those days I tried to find the spiritual side of me. I was not as strong as I once was. I am not sure if it was because a part of me was still hurt from the fact that I went through a divorce, or because I kept falling and getting back up. I know the word says we are to repent daily, but I could not understand why I kept failing the same test. When I would fall down, of course because of sin, I was so far away from God. At times it was like a part of me always longed for him when I would get caught up in situations that I knew he was not pleased with. Through his grace and mercy, he allowed me to find my way back home.

I remember this song at my old church at Faith Temple in Lawton, Oklahoma this one brother would sing, and it talked about the importance of always praying for each other because, "it might be Sister Turner trying to come home."

You never know what any child of God may be going through at any point and time. Instead of talking about them, lying about them, we should simply pray for them. None of us are exempt from trials and tribulations. None of us are exempt from falling and making wrong decisions. The word of God says to pray for one another lest the same thing falls upon you. We never know what may be ahead for us. I can say that with great conviction because of my own personal journey. I also knew that in this life there will be failure and successes throughout every aspects of our life.

Throughout these valley low and mountain high experiences I still had to be a mother. I still had to provide for them and go to parent teacher meetings, buy school clothes, take off from work because someone was ill, or in trouble at school. Parenting is a 24 hour job! I was determined my children would have the things they needed (not always the things they wanted) and that I would always surround them in love. However, it was not always easy, especially with having a teenage son, a teen parent and two intermediate age children. We had our moments, but at the end of the day we had each other. I was also blessed in that my brother relocated to Texas so that I would have a blood relative here. I had a very small circle of friends that supported me as well. It was good having others to be there for me and my children. My children gave me strength to move on because I always wanted to be someone they could look up to. In order to do that, I showed them. I showed them if you work hard and do well it will come back to you in spite of the troubles of life. I went back to school and earned my first Masters in Human Resources Management while working a full time job.

I knew I always wanted to help abused women, so I researched different organizations and programs that I could volunteer for and came across The Family Place. I volunteered at their Abused Women's Shelter. It helped me to help others. I worked with them for about a year and then I joined an organization that helped in my healing and growth. In 2007, I became a facilitator for ANTHEM Strong Families. I did relationship classes for families and eventually engaged and married couples. I fell in love with this organization and the tools I used to become healthier and stronger in my relationships. My day job was one I loved as a Contact Center Trainer and I worked with ANTHEM on some weekends. I decided to become a better me; I also had to know what I wanted and love me for who I was, flaws and all. I learned that no one can define who I was to become, but me. I decided that the new me would use my voice and be the strong universal Black woman (which is another book/dispelling the myth)!

I have used my voice in a more positive way by encouraging people and showing them through my own life that you are your biggest fan and if you do not take care of you, you cannot blame others for not doing so. I had to increase my own self-esteem about Mia. I reinvented myself. This is one of the beauties of life. If you do not like whom you are you can change! You have to show people how to treat you. Sometimes we give the power over our life to other people. These people may or may not know you, nor do they respect you. They say what they think you want to hear, only to be able to get inside of your head and turn you against you. It is so important to make sure that you are prayerfully doing the things in life you are supposed to do and that you are paying very close attention to those around you. You would be surprised at the people who actually are not for you, your growth, or your success. These individuals are strategically placed in your life to be a distraction and sometimes a dream stealer and killer. For we know the enemy comes to steal, kill and destroy by any means necessary. Life is a struggle, but only if we allow it to be. We have to understand that all of our experiences that we face come not only for us, but for someone else. Someone will come along one day going through exactly what you have gone through and you will be able to tell them look what God did for me. What he does for one he will do for another. You may be in the shoes I was in so many years ago. Heartbroken, lost, confused just in a state of shock. Having questions like why me? I have done everything that I am supposed to do! I just don't understand! Know that there is life after divorce. It's not easy and depending on how much you have invested in the marriage; it can consume you. You have to find some things in this life that are worth living for and pushing past the hurt. Even if it is to selfishly prove to the person that divorced or hurt you that you can and will succeed with or without them and do it! I can't guarantee that every day will be easy, but I can guarantee that as long as you can get back up on your feet and stand with your feet firmly planted; you can keep moving one step at a time at your own pace.

On June 16, 2013, I married my King, Mr. Pedro Whitley. He has been the man I prayed for whenever the Lord saw fit for me to marry again. I do not take this blessing lightly. I am forever grateful to the Lord for smiling on me. We both have similar testimonies and were blessed to have a beautiful dream wedding with my dad giving me away at the age of 45. Dreams come true at all ages. Phenomenal? Yes, that's me and I am still standing!

CHAPTER 4

WALKING THROUGH THE SHADOWS OF DEATH

Joyce Petry Montgomery

"Where there is hope, there is faith. Where there is faith, miracles happen."

'YEA THOU I walk through the valley of the shadows of death I will fear no evil".

How many times have I recited those words? How many times have I spoken those words? It is a very popular Psalms. We learned it as children; the 23rd Psalms. Yes, it is one of the first things we learned in Sunday school. I never would have thought that those words would have been more than just a bible scripture. I thought they were words to bring us comfort during a hard time. I thought this was just a popular scripture to recite, something just to hold on to when times were hard and I needed to know God was there. I never thought I would actually walk through the valley of the shadows of death. But I have!

MY BEGINNING

My name is Joyce M. Petry Montgomery and this is my story. I was born in October 1967 in Oberlin, Louisiana. I am the seventh child of eight children; 7 girls and 1 handsome boy. I had a happy childhood, because we were taught to love each other despite our differences. We were extremely poor but we had the best gift that outweighs being poor...we had LOVE! We have the best mother in the world. I am a very positive person and I love the Lord with all my heart and soul. I have always been a different child, quiet and to myself. My sisters and brother always teased me, because I played school all the time in our bedroom, I liked being the Teacher. I am "A" Phenomenal Woman and my story will tell you why.

WIFE, MOTHER AND WORK

I was twenty-one years old when I got married; I was told that I could not have children. Well, God had a different plan. I was blessed to birth two of the most amazing children, Joshua and Joycelyn. That was the first sign that proved to me that "God" does WHAT God WANTS to DO! My children and I have a close bond; we have wonderful relationships. I am so grateful to God that He allowed me to be a mother. My marriage was not always a happy one, but it was a decent one; and I remained faithful because my commitment is to God first and then my husband. There were times that I put my husband first because I tried to be the best wife that I could be. I put on my "Big Girl" dress and went on for years pretending that I was happy because I thought I was supposed to hang in there through thick and thin. I accepted Christ when I was fourteen years old and I thought that is what "Good" wives do. Then one day I realized that it wasn't a healthy marriage for me or my children. God saved us; I never gave up and just kept on praying. A lot of women do not see themselves as the Princesses God made us to be.

We attended a wonderful church, took vacations, but again I was going through the motions; I knew I wasn't happy. I was tolerating my life and I keep getting this feeling that life could become better. It actually became worse, my husband and I divorced after the children got older; just when I did not think it could get any worse, it did! I would have never imagined that I was going to be single parent. I was and I did what was needed to take care of my babies.

My background professionally is in mortgage and it has been rewarding for me. I worked in the mortgage industry for many years, then that ended. I prayed and asked God to please help me; I had to solely lean and depend on the Lord. I also prayed and asked God to please get me out of debt, but I didn't know how he was going to do it, but I had FAITH that he would and little did I know that He would. I tell you more about that later in the story.

My Dark Days Began and my Bright Days Returned

In August 2010, I had been in terrible pain, mainly my side. I decided to go to the emergency room; they ran all types of test on me. They said I pulled a muscle because I had just started working out. They wrote me several prescriptions for pain medications and sent me home, which was the first time. The pain got worse and I returned to the emergency room, this time they decided to put a scope into my stomach to find out what was going on. Dr. A. was determined to find the cause of my pain.

34

Little did I know at the time that Dr. A. was "God sent"! The other doctor wanted to send me home again with additional pain pills. They took me into surgery that afternoon and here is where my life changed.

My sisters told me Dr. A. came out of surgery and told them that I had cancer. He knew that it was cancer but wasn't sure which one, he was positive that it was not Breast or Ovarian cancer. They all sound pretty bad, right? My sisters, Pat, Barbara, Dora, Leona, and my daughter Joycelyn, tried to protect me and our mother for 4 days. They were waiting until the pathology report was confirmed that it was cancer. It was cancer and a very "Big" one called Mesothelioma. The name was impossible to pronounce; we should have known then that it was deadly, a name like that had to be bad. Mesothelioma is a rare cancer; most people generally get it from exposure to asbestos. This type of cancer is usually found in the lungs, the stomach or the heart. The tumor was in my stomach and had spread to my liver. We were told it was Stage 4; there is no other stage after 4. This looked like the end!

I literally saw my life disappearing. I cried out to God many times asking why He allowed this to happen to me; I was thinking I had been faithful to my church and His word. God had a plan and I decided to go to WAR! I started speaking the word of God and reminding God of His own word. Not that He needs reminders; I knew God knew His word, but I wanted Him to know that I knew His Word. I spoke Isaiah 53:5 "By HIS stripes I am healed".

My family, my friends and I were devastated that I was diagnosed with cancer. In June 2008, Shonda, our baby sister, died due to breast cancer and she was only 38 years old. My family could not handle the news of another daughter or sister having cancer; you automatically think of death even though our Mom, Ms. Willie M. Petry is a 29 year Breast cancer Survivor. Go Mom, you are our Warrior Queen! They just could not believe the doctors were telling them that I had cancer.

I prayed and asked God to bless me with some great doctors and He did just that, Dr. B is not only handsome; he is one of the best cancer surgeons. I had major surgery on December 9th and I was in the hospital for

9 days. My big brother slept in the waiting room all 9 days to be with me. They removed almost all of the lining in my stomach and burned the small tumors on my liver. As I mentioned, I was told that I was in Stage 4 of the cancer. If you know anything about cancer that ISN'T WHAT YOU WANT TO HEAR!! And to make matters worse the Palliative care Doctor was sent to my hospital room. I'm sure most of you do not know who or what Palliative care is. I didn't know however, my sister dealt with the Palliative care team when Shonda (our baby sister) was in the hospital. Palliative Care is for people who are seriously or terminally ill, they provide care from a physical, mental and emotional standpoint to reduce stress and improve the quality of life. In other words let me give you a little education here: The Palliative Care Doctor is the one that comes in after they tell you that you only have a certain amount of time to LIVE! My sisters knew of this appointment and they had planned a "Tag Team", making sure that someone would be with me at all times. Well low and behold the PD arrived early and all hell broke loose. The PD told me that the doctors had done all that they could do and basically I was going to die. I was shocked, numb, terrified and was staring at the lady with my mouth open thinking MY SISTERS DID NOT TELL ME I WAS DYING!! I called Leona, screaming and crying asking why was I going to die and why didn't she tell me? It was horrible, the poor girl in the bed next to me who had just had a baby, was crying with me. Leona called the Sister Posse' and they all headed my way. And they were very angry that the PD arrived early. NO ONE should have to go through this alone my siblings are PROTECTORS! When Le arrived the first thing she asked me to do was look at my feet. I'm thinking I'm dying and she wants me to look at my feet? I did and she asked me did I see a "Toe Tag" that they put on the person when someone dies. I told her NO, I didn't see one.

She told me to take a deep breath, stop crying and listen to her; she reminded me that *only God* knows our death date and until He tells us the date we need to keep on living! She promised me that I was not going to die. My Sister Posse' arrived and prayed like never before and I started to smile again. But Palliative Care Physicians will scare the life out of you.

WATCH GOD WORK

Again, they told me Stage 4! This is the stage where man throws up his hands and says "Think about your quality of life"! Basically saying "let us just make you comfortable because really; it is too late!"

BUT GOD!!!

In God's eyes it is a very different view point. This is the time when God says, "Man has done all that he can now move back and watch ME WORK!

I started praying and asking God for a complete healing in my body. I am a true believer in His Word and I stood on FAITH that I was going to be healed! Remembering the words of Isaiah 53:5!

December I started taking chemotherapy; it was not an easy battle. I give kudos to all Warriors that go through chemo. I knew that I had to stand on my faith and believe with all my heart that God was going to do what I ask God to do in my life. The first treatment almost took me out! It was very hard, it felt like I was losing my mind and didn't know where I was. I started praying to God reminding Him of HIS Word again, telling him that I couldn't take this chemo and I wanted a complete healing in my body.

Being hooked up to an IV that is pumping medicine in you that kill the cancer cells but it also kills the healthy cells seems crazy, but necessary. So you body is out of whack. Chemo comes with pain, mouth sores, hair loss, skin issues, and finger and toe nail issues. You body is being depleted of everything it needs and you are fighting to get food in you when you don't want to eat it. You are trying to drink when you don't want to drink. Your bones hurt, you feel weak, you are miserable, sometimes nauseated, wanting the process to be over and done with. Then you have to look at yourself, you either lose weight, gain weight, all the hair on your body is gone. You see the wind blowing you hair right off your head or you wake up it is on your pillow or in the shower. You don't feel attractive and you have to be creative. You are now the center of attention. All eyes are on you. Some people are wondering if you are going to die, others wondering when will you die. Your children are afraid for you; one child embraces you the other child is in denial and struggling with the concept. You really cannot comfort them because you are trying to just keep your food down and the pain at bay.

In all that I knew that I had to continue to stand on my faith on what I ask God to do in my life. I could not give in now. I had invested too much in prayer, too much time in the throne room. I had to keep going; I had to walk through this! As I was looking at my sister Leona, in my mind I didn't know if I could continue the chemo. This was horrible! It was! I constantly reminded myself, I know a MAN that is BETTER and STRONGER than chemo and His name is JESUS CHRIST. While they were administering the chemo I knew I had to focus on His word.

I understand people with this type of cancer live for an average of 10 to 18 months. I knew then that I had work to do, so I went into my secret closet and I prayed to God asking Him if He would heal my body; that I would share my experience with the world. I would tell everyone everywhere I go that God is still performing miracles. I made a vow to the Lord that if He healed my body I would not shut up telling the world about Him. And to this day I'm talking louder and sharing God's Word and my testimony. A quote that I said to myself was, "I have cancer but cancer, DOES NOT have me. God has me!" I meant every word of that and so the fight began with my journey of cancer.

January 2011 one of my sisters took me to the doctor for my check up, but before then I was praying and asking God to heal my body because I did not want to continue having chemo treatments. I was told that I had to take 4 to 6 rounds of chemo for six months. Well the oncologist came in the room and started talking to me and stated that my pathology report came back and there were NO more cancer cells and I did not have to take anymore chemo. Boy was I the happiest woman in the world; then and there I started thanking God, because He answered my prayers. What an AWESOME God I serve!!!

During these very dark moments in my life I met a young man, by the name of Corey that was very affectionate and attentive to me. While in my darkness he was a ray of sunshine. He was with me through the surgery, chemotherapy and being bald. This was his first time experiencing this and he had no idea what to expect, but he was not leaving my side. Afterward he told me that he had been praying; asking God not to take me from him. Honesty, I was not trying to hear it. I was just getting over a bad marriage and now trying to hold on for dear life battling cancer.

As of today I am four years cancer free and I am mentoring and speaking to others that are battling with cancer. Because I know that God gave me a second chance; for this reason I LOVE to share my testimony whenever I get a chance. I love the opportunity to uplift, encourage, and empower others with the Word of God. I encourage them to keep a positive attitude, trust, believe and keep the faith and they will make it through their battle.

As I mention earlier, I prayed and asked God to bless my finances and He did! He blessed me to purchase a cash home and three cars, one for each child and one for myself. *WITH GOD ALL THINGS ARE POSSIBLE!!*

I have met several ladies that are battling cancer. I mentored one special lady; she is a God-sent friend. I had the opportunity to walk with her through her journey of battling breast cancer and it was truly an amazing experience. God allowed me to take her under my wing and pray with her, encourage her and share my story as well. I enjoy what God has placed in my heart to do; you have to go through a journey in order to help someone else along their journey. I have had the opportunity to speak on a Christian Internet Channel, Gospel Radio and in different churches. I also told part of my story in a gospel magazine. I do not take any credit for this; I give God ALL the praise, honor, and glory.

I thank God for my loving husband, God has blessed me with, married for three years and he has been supportive. I also give major thanks to my wonderful children, mother, sisters, my brother and all my extended family and friends for being so supportive. Thanks to my Pastor,

Co-Pastor and church family for their support. I am an active member and dedicated to the Faith Counselor, Voices of Judah, Hospitality and Women's Ministry. I love being a Christian in the Kingdom of God.

I pray that my story empowers many lives and help encourage anyone that is battling with cancer or any disease, that they will trust, believe and have faith in God and BELIEVE they are healed by His stripes. I give God all the praise, honor, and glory. I thank God for allowing me to share "Walking through the Shadows of Death". My journey causes me look at life total differently. I no longer things for granted. I believe this valley experience is the reason, I am phenomenal! I know it is the reason I still stand!

CHAPTER 5

AFTER ALL THIS, I AM STILL PHENOMENAL

Dr. Sarah Ransom

"Before you can touch a life, you must feel their pain."

"I count not myself to have apprehended, but this one thing I do, forget-ting those things which are behind, and REACHING forth unto those things which are before or ahead of me, I PRESS toward the mark for the prize of the high calling of God in Christ Jesus". Phil 3:13-14 KJV

A MOTHER OF 3 beautiful children: LaToya, Jasmine and Christian and a grandmother of 2 precious grandchildren: Prince Alaiya (6) and Prince Isaiah (9mos). I am BLESSED!

My journey started years ago making me the *"Phenomenal Woman"* that I am today. I owe God, first and then my incredible parents, the Late William Ransom and my loving mother, Margaret Ransom, who is yet with us at the gracious age of 76. Of course, there are many other great people I owe "Thanks" to—such as pastors, professors, teachers, instructors, leaders, colleagues and peers. I always say that I am the sum total of so many people who have poured into my life along the way. Each one of them imparted something inside of me to help pave, direct and empower me to be this, *"Phenomenal Woman"*!

Purpose began long before time was. However, it was manifested on earth when my parents decided to have pleasure. Being the middle child of eight children, I was gifted to see and observe siblings born before and after me. What a wonderful position to be in—the middle.

Things have not been easy for me, but I always look at the solution, rather than the problem. I take condescending messages and usually prove them to be the opposite of who I am in Christ. The Holy Spirit has been a constant and consistent friend and confidant in my life now for decades. I owe all that I am and shall be to HIM.

I lost my Dad at the tender age of 12 years old. It was my first great loss. Oh! How it seemed to have been a tragedy that I didn't think that I would overcome, but I did with the help of God and His Holy Word. It did not happen overnight. I grieved for 15 years –many mistakes and wrong decisions I made all because of emotional pain and trauma. That's why I can spot a "hurting" heart and a "wounded" spirit in a split second. There are signs and actions that prove hurt lives behind the scenes in the lives of the hurting. It just cannot be faked or hidden. My family and I stuck together, even after the full circle of family was broken. We had no one to lean on but God and each other. Did we have our challenges? Yes! Indeed—but we did not let them stop us from succeeding in life. At the tender age of 11, I was teaching my Dad to read and to write. For Dad dropped out of school in the fourth grade to support his family because his Dad had an illness that would not let him work. He was a drunk; but grandmother loved him, until the day she died. Amazingly, he died a few months later.

I love ministering to the Body of Christ. Although, I know I have a "unique" style but I am just Who I Am. I cannot be anyone other than what God made me. I celebrate all the wonderful married couples who have held on and are holding on. Marriage is work and ministry! I must not forget those who have made a choice, to perhaps, clean up what was messed up and started life over again. We often hear the scripture, "What therefore God hath joined together let not man put asunder". I firmly believe this, but take notice, every marriage God doesn't join together. Sometimes, flesh does. Situations do, circum-stances do or people do! 1984, I moved to the Dallas Forth Worth area and from there my life began to change. I met my husband in June 1985, and we later married. God showed me in a dream that I would have two daughters and they would be as we call, "stair-step"; a year or so apart. They both had on little white satin dresses and appeared in my bedroom as "little angels". It scared me because I had never seen God showing me something like that about my future. I was not think-ing about children or marriage at the time. Well, LaToya was born July 1988 and Jasmine June 1989, 11 months and nine days later. My hands were full with two precious busy little girls. We worked for them and always wanted them to have the best. I dressed them like twins for so long until many people to this day, think they are twins! I am so amazed at their level of maturity at this stage in their lives. LaToya and her husband Jonathan and two precious children are a blessing to our family and friends. Jasmine has always been the softer one, but strong in her own right. The two girls are so smart and intelligent. There are things I learn from them as much as they do from me. Christian came and put the icing on the cake and gave BALANCE to us all! He holds his grandmother, Margaret Ransom's spirit; kind and loving towards all people, everywhere.

In 1988, I married my friend I had known for a few years. We had some wonderful times. God blessed us beyond measures; financially, materially, socially, economically—we became so blessed until the enemy got mad. My husband, at the time, lost his Dad and I noticed we started encountering all kinds of problems. He was so hurt, confused and bitter. I'm sure it was because he was there visiting his Dad at home when he started having a heart attack. This seemed to be a reoccurring sight and scene that would play over and over again in his mind. Death is a spirit and it leaves a lot of brokenness to those who are left behind. People take things differently. What is the right way to take deep pain and hurt? Most people still today are seeking ways to heal from something that left them breathless and paralyzed in life.

In 1995, my husband and I, received the shock of our lives; the news of a third child after I had a tubal ligation, which is supposed to be a form of permanent birth control. At the time, our second daughter, Jasmine was 6 years old and in first grade. We thought we were DONE! We were finished having children. Well! God had a different plan. So, again, I went through an emotional time in my life having to accept the will of God. God had showed me in a dream a few years before, having a son at home. I was hoping this dream (unlike others) was not real. Well, after my nine month experience carrying him with everyone so excited about it, except for me; I had to realize that my life was not my own and that God had a purpose for Christian Henry. He was born (at home through a midwife) on March 21, 1996. Christian is an amazing child. He loves God and people. He's a lot like his Dad, Ronald "Bo" Henry.

In the year of 2000, I was diagnosed with a terrible respiratory and lung condition. I thought my life was over. Some of what I was going through was demonic. If I were not gifted as a seer; I would not have known what was going on. In the daytime, I'd be under severe attacks where I could not breathe and my chest was so sore, it felt as if it was closing in. I was given an inhaler, which put extreme weight on my body. Since that day until 2015, I have had to fight the weight gain and condition. There were times I went to the doctor and hated getting on the scale. Of course, I carried my weight well. At night, God would show me preaching, teaching and prophesying to thousands in various cities and nations. He gave me this word: "If you don't prophesy, they will die. If you don't give, they won't live!" Since that time, I have been releasing prophetic revelations and utterances almost on a daily basis to many. I had an out-of-body experience that changed my life forever. I know what it is like to die; it took about 2 minutes to actually pass from earth to heaven. I entered this path, it was a light there and as I got closer to where the light led me to it was a bright light like I have never seen before on this earth. It was a spiritual light! I saw Jesus and He was smiling, but shortly after, I returned back to earth all this took about 2-5 minutes to experience. I learned then, that death is REAL, but I was not afraid. There was so much peace and there was such a presence as if someone (in which it was), was with me! It was Jesus! It was somewhat hard to come back and go through life after having that kind of experience.

Years later, I am standing and I noticed that there was a heavier anointing released upon my life. Also in the year of 2000, the Holy Spirit also gave me this word when I was sick unto death. He said: "You shall lay hands on the sick and they shall recover." I thought to myself: I guess I will if I ever make it through this! Well! I made it out and alright full of passion and with my praise. I never lost my praise even in the darkest place in my life. My Praise was life and light to me.

Then in the year of 2005 I experienced another dreadful time in my life, a Divorce! Wow! Me? Thought it would never be. During the process of an almost two year divorce, I went through some traumatizing and emotional upheavals. I could feel God's presence surrounding me through this life changing transition. There were days, I felt numb, without any feeling. I was so full of disappointment, hurt and pain. I felt God for a moment, but I had to come back. He was constantly and consistently pulling and tugging at my heart. I was ministering (teaching and singing) to others while so broken on the inside. My nights were bitter and long, my days were too short. I experienced seemingly a "Wrong Hand" as card player would say. Through fasting, prayer and continuously study of the Word; I beat and defied the odds of a 40 year old divorcee who had been "faithfully and devoted" to one man for 20 years. I look back at it all now and see that God was just moving me into a "higher" place in Him and in Ministry. I often say, "You cannot minister effectively where you have not been yourself!" I used to say that there were two things you do only once and that is to, "Get Saved" and "Get Married"! Well, saved is true, but the saying concerning marriage is no longer valid. As I am planning to give this wonderful covenant a try and chance again. For I know it is God's will as He has confirmed it in my Spirit.

I have a great passion for the broken. I, too, have been broken in life so much to the point that I thought that I would never gain soundness ever again. BUT GOD! There are far too many fairy tales that some people live by, until a great storm comes and knock them out of the boat! It's okay for the boat to be in the water. But it becomes dangerous when the water gets in the boat. I call this Life! There will be storms in life, no matter how you sing, preach, teach and pray. It is part of our growth and it is certainly part of our Testimony.

Sometimes, our story might not touch everybody, but it is sure to touch some. I realize that I am called by God to do a work and as long as I am still here my purpose is not complete. I've learned you don't have to be bound. You can be free in Him! God's will is that we live the Abundant Life as He intended and planned for us. I am in a safe place with God. I live a life of much prayer and my daily regime is first spiritual and then, natural. Keeping it this way keeps me balanced. I just wouldn't trade my life now, for anything or anybody that's not called to celebrate my victory!

It would be safe to say, that I have fought through some dreadful times and events in my life and yet have a passion and love for God and His people. I see the best under the surface of most people. This is the eye of a seer. We see but we also help perfect those things that are causing many to lose ground in God. I have lost numerous love ones along the way as well. This hurts my heart! I still can hear and see many things that each one of them said to encourage me as a young girl and a young lady growing up in life and ministry. I have always had a "strong", can't break me-type of character. God placed this inside of me early in life. I was a tomboy growing up. I was rough, running through the grass, turning cart wheels and backwards flips with no hands. I could have been an Acrobat had I pursued it. I certainly enjoyed my childhood to the fullest. We were raised, for a period of time, in the country hills. I am well acquainted with the different types of wildlife. Quite interesting!!!

I'm moving into another era in my life, after raising my children and being a devoted Mom and (yet one) to them. It seems a bit strange because for years, I was so consumed with mothering, schooling; homework, sports, band, choir and extra-curricular activities. It came upon me so fast. I am so proud of my children. Of course, we have had our challenges, like most families do. We're a family who believes in prayer and that there is nothing GOD cannot do! Now, I am resting in the peace of GOD! I can dedicate more of my time to Him versus having to divide my time with a husband (at one time), and three children. I realize God gives each one of us what we can handle through HIM! I can't say my life was all bad---there have been more good days, than bad! I am just a grateful person and I always have been. I firmly believe God will never harm or hurt me and won't allow others for too long! I consider myself a blessed and highly favored individual. Not because I chose to be, but because HE chose me! I honor the life God has given to me and I try my best to walk it out and please HIM! Of course, He and I have constant talks about many things. I just love to hear Him minister to my spirit. I can be down and out and He will come and say things like: "Daughter, I love you!" or, "I got this"! Those types of words from God are like music to my ears. I can't live, can't breathe, and can't move without HIM!

In the year 2016, many prophecies will come to pass in my life. Some prophecies were spoken 10, 20 and 30 years ago. I see God's hands upon my every move. He certainly orders my steps. (Psalm 37:23 KJV) One of my favorite passages of scripture is found in Ephesians 3:20,21 KJV: "Now unto HIM (God), that is able to do exceeding abundantly above all that we ask or think, according to the power that worketh in us, 21) Unto HIM be glory in the church by Christ Jesus throughout all ages, world without end. Amen." I have lived by this scripture for well over 25 years. Each time I have a hard challenge or a turn in my life, I stand on these passages of scripture. God always supersedes my expectations.

Where would I be without the Lord? I don't want to think about it. I owe Him my all. My all, I owe HIM! God has been a friend, companion, confidant, father, doctor, lawyer, mind regulator and the list is endless. I hold in high regard my relationship with the Lord, first and then those I hold dear thereafter. I look back over the years of my life and I can truly say God has been with me all the way. At times, when I thought I wouldn't make it, recover or come through. God was there! I could feel His presence, even in my darkest hour.

I love the parable of The Talents in Matthew 25:14-30 KJV...the part that really gain my attention is the one who went and hid his (ONE) talent in the earth....His lord said unto him: "Thou wicked and slothful servant, thou knewest that I reap where I sowed not, and gather where I have not strawed, Thou oughtest therefore to have put my money to the exchangers, and then at my coming I should have received mine own usury. Take therefore the talent (FROM) him, and give it unto him which hath ten talents. For unto everyone that hath shall be given, and he shall have abundance: but from him that hath not shall be (TAKEN AWAY) even that which he hath. This tells me that God holds us to a higher level of accountability for what He has given to each one of us. Not only is He watching to see what we do, but if what we do is FRUITFUL and that it MULTIPLIES. He gave this command in Genesis

1:28 KJV: "And God blessed them (male and female), and God said unto them, "Be fruitful, and multiply, and replenish the earth, and subdue it", and have dominion over the fish of the sea, and over the fowl of the air, and over every living thing, that moveth upon the earth."

I am not Extraordinary, Outstanding or Remarkable for any reason. It's all because of great purpose. God has graced me with multiple gifts and talents, and I wouldn't think of hiding not one of them—because a "Phenomenal Woman" cannot be hidden. Her light shines so bright--bringing love, inner strength, healing and hope to wherever she goes. That's ME-a Phenomenal Woman indeed!

CHAPTER 6

INTERRUPTION OF THE PLAN

Kendra Dee

"When obstacles arise, you change your direction to
reach your goal- you do not change your decision to get
there. " ~Zig Ziglar

"INTERRUPTION OF THE PLAN"

Running late from a meeting on a balmy summer night, I could not wait to get home to my kids, and my new husband, Joseph, of 7 ½ months! In the excitement about the new job that I was starting the next day. I rushed up the stairs to our apartment to find my son sitting on the couch watching TV, and my daughter and husband in the bedrooms. I kissed my son, hugged my daughter, kissed my husband, and joined him in our bedroom.

Joseph asked me about my day, as I did of him. As we spoke briefly, I noticed that Joseph's mind was somewhere else – his job often stressed him out, so I chose not to question him any further. I took a shower, and then rejoined him in the bedroom. When I returned, Joseph already had laid back down. He raised his head, kissed me, told me that he loved me, turned off the lamp, and we both went to sleep. 10:59 p.m., Tuesday night...

"What is that movement?"....

I sat straight up in the bed and looked at the clock... 5:42 a.m... I turned to my right to see the silhouette of my husband in a fetal position, shaking uncontrollably, his arms as stiff as boards. Assuming that he was having a dream, I shoved him in the shoulder, through a yawn, *"baby, wake up"*... The shaking continued; the sounds coming from Joseph were as if he was wheezing or couldn't breathe... More alert at this time, I spoke a little louder and shoved his shoulder a little harder. *"Baby, wake up, wake up"* ... I screamed, *"Joseph, wake up, wake up!!"*... My hand touched his face – saliva was on his chin and the tip of his tongue was sticking out of his mouth... The shaking stopped... 5:43 a.m.... I hurried back to my side of the bed, turned on the lamp, and slowly turned my head again to the right side of the bed...

Panic, shock, disbelief, fear, confusion flooded my mind at once. Frantic and scared, I managed to call the paramedics and told them what happened, as I tried to revive my husband. I lifted his left arm, and watched in horror as it fell back on the bed with no resistance. I checked his wrist, chest, and his neck - no heartbeat, no pulse, no breathing. As tears filled my eyes, the paramedics arrived. Their noisy, bold entrance and rushed movements alarmed my daughter, who watched her new step-father be taken out of the house on a stretcher to the ambulance. My son awoke as I rushed to get dressed to follow the ambulance to the hospital.

When I arrived, I was led to the ER and into the room where the staff was trying tirelessly to revive Joseph. As I watched in horror everything that was happening, a part of me thought I was watching a 3D movie, up close and personal to a theater screen – but this was no theatrical production; it was my reality. With tears in my eyes and shock in my face, I slowly approached the left side of Joseph, and shoved his shoulder for what would be the last time, and said with a cracking voice, "*baby, wake up*". One of the nurses, as professionally empathetic as she could be at that time, said those six words confirming that life as I knew it was over – *"I'm sorry. Your husband is gone…"*

I looked at her in shock and disbelief. *"What do you mean, GONE?"* The room began to spin. I fell back into a chair that had been placed behind me. Breathing was difficult. I gently rubbed his cheek with the back of my hand – no response. I grabbed his hand and dropped it as if I were burnt by a flame – it was cold. *This was not happening to me,* I told myself. It was too soon. We had plans. He was too young… and I was supposed to start a new job that day… I hesitantly picked up his lifeless hand again, rested my head on his thigh, tears rolling down my face… I was soon summoned by the nurses to speak to the hospital chaplain… Joseph was dead.

The first few nights without Joseph were terrifying. I did not know if I was coming or going. My mind played tricks on me and was on edge. I could smell his scent everywhere… Questions flood-ed my brain, not to mention the roller-coaster that my emotions were on. Rest was a rare pleasure, and sleep was a luxury that I needed but did not welcome due to the dreams I had about Joseph. The tormenting images in my night hours were often too much.

My first night on the sofa was nothing short of restless. I stared at my cellphone all night, expecting Joseph to call me and tell me that this was all a joke, that he was waiting for me at the Medical Examiner's office. I repeatedly rehearsed his words in my head – *"Hey baby. I am finished here at the ME's office... It is too late to catch the bus, so please come get me... why did you leave me here alone?!... Please don't leave me alone..."* I can recall several nights that I would see Joseph attempting to claw himself out of his white casket, begging for help and using the little air he had until the mounds of dirt smothered his face... The fearful vision of opening the bedroom closet and seeing him standing there, in his ragged burial clothes, with fresh autopsy scars... The frequent thoughts of him walking down a dark street like a zombie, after escaping the casket, heading back to our home... Oh, yeah, it was rough!

It did not take me long to bury myself deep inside my cave, my safe place. *Who in their right mind would want to deal with this,* I wondered. The struggle with the personal acceptance of this realistic twilight zone was difficult enough, not to mention being an example of "what to do" as my children watched me. Every single thing that they had seen as a sign of strength, resilience, and positivity in their mother was standing on rocky ground. *Who would be their rock now*? I had no more to give, I could no longer pretend that I had it all together because I did not. This burden, this weight was too much, even for a pillar like me. I had grown so accustomed to being the Leaned On, that I felt lost as the one who needed to lean on someone else. It was strange, scary, and uncertain. I had no idea that I was about to live the words I had heard across the pulpit for years – *"My grace is sufficient for you, for My power is made perfect in weakness."*

The process was arduous, the days were unpredictable, and there were times when fear of the unknown was so strong that I made progress or took actions with my eyes closed. I began to notice and appreciate the little things, the small steps or acts that used to seem so insignificant under normal circumstances. Closure began to take place – I was able to go through Joseph's belongings... I could look at pictures of us without being afraid of the tears that were faithful to follow... talking about that fateful day was easier, minus the feelings of guilt that used to torment me... People who were not meant to walk this portion of my journey with me began to drop off. Yes, *when someone dies, you will be shocked by the ones who love you, despise you, support you, and reject you" ... No truer words have ever been spoken, and no truer words have ever been proven in a time of loss and pain more than these.*

As the weeks turned into months, I was able to function with the brokenness in my life. I had reached the limit of the uncomfortableness in my comfort zone, and subconsciously vowed never to cross that line. After all, who would want to keep riding the wild, uncontrollable ride of the emotional roller-coaster that so boldly graced my life with its unwanted presence or reality? However, something happened on the inside of me. I was reawakened. I cannot pinpoint the exact date, time or event, but suddenly, I saw life in a different perspective, and I realized that I was simply alive and no longer living. I had come to the place where I had to make the decision that would transform the world as I knew it – do I stay in this broken place and die with my late husband or do I take the first step to continue to live? Do I selfishly waddle in my pain and use it as a crutch with justifiable woe – or do I embrace the process of the pain and allow myself and my children to be healed? One decision would make me feel better (if only for a while), but one would make me BE better... and that is the one I chose...

What a season – the walk of a widow! Never in my life had I experienced such depths of pain, change, hurt, disappointment, pruning, and self-examination. A spotlight that you cannot flee and a process you cannot rush or skip through! Mere words cannot begin to properly or worthily describe the lessons, revelations, and truths that I learned during this time. However, there is one thing I saw for sure - *During the darkest minute of your darkest hour, a deep-seeded source of unexplainable, undeniable, & unshakable strength and peace becomes available to you, which will get you through that place. No matter the pain, sorrow, or agony that is indeed justified, waddling in the "woe-is-me" of that place will not change or bring back what was lost, so let the Comforter and Healer be who & what He is. You will see that this may be your greatest - or possibly only source of strength...*

If you are in this place, I know the pain and emptiness it causes. But I also know that Life is not over. There is life after death. While mourning the sudden loss of Joseph and in my attempt to struggle through the indescribable hurt, there was no doubt that my mental and emotional "end" was closing in on me – yet, to my surprise, I was awakened to a new beginning. I learned, through pain and revelation, that there was more life after Joseph than there was before him...

I learned more about who Kendra really was than what I had known the 30-something years prior to widowhood. There were things inside of me that were untapped, suppressed, broken, and hidden, due to the challenges I faced early in life, and the manner that I chose to respond to and process the pain that derived from my current trials, including widowhood. I was indeed transforming into a new creation – the old Kendra was passing away and a new one was emerging. If you have never lost someone so close (spouse, parent, or child), it may be difficult for you to understand the depths of this level of growth, faith, and strength, but it is real. It takes work – and your active participation.

Have you ever baked a cake, from scratch? Do you remember your first successful attempt? You had all of the ingredients ready – the flour, eggs, and so on – and put it in the oven. You knew that the cake was going to turn out delicious, but before it reached its perfected state, it had to endure the process of mixture, heart, and cooking. Now, you could have put the cake in the oven, walked away, and returned when it was done, but you, being so proud of each cake you make, decided to sit in the kitchen, turn on the oven light, and watch your cake go through the process. You did not take the cake out of the oven or turn off the heat until all of the combined ingredients made the perfected product...

So it is with our lives and the process of restoration. As with the cake, it cannot be baked on a low temperature; the oven must be hot and heated well so that our "cake mix" (our trials, tragedies, challenges) will be cook perfectly and yield a perfected cake. Of course, the heat of the oven doesn't feel good, and it is definitely something we would rather conceal or pretend is nonexistent. Mind as well submit to the process, though - we will not be taken out of the oven until we make the right sound or come out 'clean' when the toothpick is inserted.

What does the description of a cake have to do with personal restoration? EVERYTHING. All of the ingredients that my cake was comprised of (yes, including widowhood) were all combined together, put into the oven, and made me who I am today. Every one of those unfortunate events could have led to my destruction, but they have worked out for my good. No longer am I trapped inside of the fortress that I built to hide the process of restoration from this pain. Sure, I am still a work in progress, as you are, but I am no longer ashamed.

One of the most challenging yet advantageous lessons I learned during this season is to accept that some things (and people) are only meant to be in your life for a season, and some are meant for a lifetime, but they all have a reason. As strange as this may sound to some who have never walked as a widow/widower, have never had a true broken experience, or who simply are unlearned or lack understandings, my late husband completed his assignment. He fulfilled his purpose in life – and I in his. I walked the path that was predestined for me to experience, so that I could become the woman that I am today. Believe me when I tell you that the Kendra who is writing this would not exist had it not been for the challenges and obstacles I not only overcame but learned from, including the one as a widow.

What?!?! Yes... *He was supposed to die and leave you as a widow?* Reality - we all have an appointed time to transition into eternity, and cannot choose when or how it is destined to manifest... *This was 'okay' with you?!* Gosh, no! Who would want Death to brazenly enter the home, snatch a loved one, with no known sickness, with no warning and in less than 60 seconds?! Please, in the heat of the battle, all I wanted to do was escape! But, as I yielded to what I could not change, and allowed my perspective to be transformed, this life-changing principle saved my soul – and I share it with you: *"Approach each territory, relationship, opportunity, and connection with the perspective of assignment and purpose. This way, you won't be __as__ distraught, disappointed, and discontent when the season with that thing (or person) ends…"*

Reminiscing on that season of my life, and the many other obstacles that I have overcame, I cannot help but smile. Indeed, the walk of a widow(er) – especially when it is unexpected and you are unprepared for it – is something that you have to "see" to believe. There were many days where I was so embarrassed with myself that I would hide from and avoid everyone, but Life has taught me that our trials, and the process of walking through them, are not about me… and yours are not about you… ***When something that was once dear to you is taken away, it becomes easier to surrender everything else because you realize that you are not in control, it is not about you - and Life and Death take on totally different meanings...***

As we continue to go forward and yield ourselves to Life, we will encounter someone (often one whom you least expect) who is in the midst of the very challenge that we have overcome, or who is still bound in their minds by the effects of it. Your honesty, empathy, and transparency can be used as a beacon of hope, faith, and confidence in the life of that person. What an honor it is to pay it forward, to influence the life of a person whose freedom and wholeness may come from ***your*** mouth!

This is the beginning of the most powerful days of your life, if you will allow it to be. Just keep walking, one step at a time… You are reading this, so that season did not kill you – it made you stronger…

The old life is no more – embrace the new…

Restoration.

CHAPTER 7

PHENOMENAL WOMAN! ME? YES ME!

Dianne "Pastor di" Matthews

"Success seems to be connected with action. Successful people keep moving. They make mistakes, but they don't quit."

— CONRAD HILTON

I NEVER WOULD have used the word Phenomenal to describe myself. I honestly would have said several other words. I would describe myself as determined, relentless, passionate, dedicated, rebellious, adventurous, fearless, considerate, sympathetic, enduring, humble to a fault, easy going and I thought maybe even extraordinary. I thought about that last word extraordinary. I am definitely not an ordinary person, not an ordinary woman. Extraordinary, yep that is me! So I settled in my mind that extraordinary really defines what kind of person I am. Yes I am an extraordinary person, an extraordinary woman. I am extraordinary! I pondered what is extraordinary? If you look at synonyms for extraordinary you find the word phenomenal. Ah! Yes! Phenomenal! I now can agree I am a phenomenal woman!

You might be thinking what is it about her that makes her so phenomenal? What makes her stand out above other women? You might think, we all have a story, so what makes her so different? I really think it is my ability to be resilient. I have that good ole bounce back in my blood! I have worked with enough people to know that sometimes we don't adapt, we don't make it through adversity, we don't come out on top; sometimes we don't come out at all. I don't have a fairy tale story, nor do I have the worst story, it is not a tearjerker, well at least not to me. It is probably like many stories, but definitely has not been a boring one. My life has been quite chaotic, pretty much all my life; since I did not know what chaos was, I never knew I was in it. It was my normal. My life has been very interesting! I have learned to understand what bizarre really means!

I was born breech birth, which is feet first, not head. I think that if I was to learn something about my birth, it was first a painful one for my mother. Secondly, I believe that "feet first "was the sign that I was destined to walk out everything in the earth. I cannot say GOD has not favored me, but I can say that I have been through much, in my eyes way too much. I finally made up my mind that GOD really likes me because He trusts me to make it through the hard test. I believe my destiny and purpose has been hard to reach, hard to get to, a very hard walk, a hard road, and one that was bumpy, full of twists, turns and trials. I think this was God's design; this way I cannot ever say that I earned it or did it on my own. I cannot say nor can anyone else say that it was laid in my lap. I have to say it was the grace of GOD that carried me through it! It was the road I had to travel to receive the promises of GOD!

I was not raised by my mother but by her sister, my aunt and her husband. I lived with them approximately seven years before I was actually adopted; I was 12 then. My parents decided on 3 children with me being the eldest. My sister and brother came through an adoption agency. I believe I was loved, I believe that my siblings were favored. I'm not bashing my parents but I have to tell this from my own feelings. I know they meant well, according to their own testimony they did the best they knew how. I seemed to stay in trouble, take the whippings even when I was not guilty. I dreamed of attending football games, participating in activities at the school that I was interested in, my mother had her own dreams for me; I wanted to do things but they were always the opposite of what she wanted. I was only able to participate in things she suggested or wanted to see me in, it was indeed her dream, her reality of my life, and it really was her show. My mother was a bit difficult, a bit strange; I guess today if she were alive and diagnosed she would be bi-polar. I could not wait to graduate. I was quiet but when I got to the eleventh grade I took the early graduate program because all I wanted to do WAS GET OUT OF THE HOUSE! I went to Houston, Texas to school. I enrolled in Texas Southern University and then the University of Houston. I was so happy to be away from home. This was okay with her because she saw it as another opportunity to live vicariously through me, but my plan was a little different, I just needed to get away from home.

I was a church girl. I accepted Christ at age 15, I had been in church all my life, participated in everything and I thought I had it all together, until I began to see people and hear the testimonies of young people who said Christ changed their life. I knew then I did not have all the facts and I learned I knew of Jesus but I did not know Him. I set out to have a close relationship, with Him. I am glad I did because I went through so many different things that if Jesus had not been a part of my life I would not be here today.

I am saved and in Houston, Texas, 16 years old. I was so not ready. I was not prepared for the world. I just wanted to get away from my family. I cannot tell the entire story but I can say I found myself in some places and situations that could have gone wrong. I must say that it was indeed the grace of GOD that kept me. I am very fortunate I was caught up in church drama, church politics and church foolishness. Oh God I thank you for deliverance, I thank you for keeping my reputation intact and I thank you for not letting me die in my sins nor die from disease because I was out there, looking for love in all the wrong places and not finding it anywhere!.

From one college to the next, I was on a journey, I am telling you there have been many steps in my life, many different cadences, and I have been marching and walking a long time trying to get somewhere. I enrolled in Texas Southern University and stayed there a year. I honestly did not like it; my upbringing and the attitude that I learned from my parents really dulled my thinking about being African American. I did not fit in. I enrolled in University of Houston, I fit a little bit better, more of my world, but the bad habits I had at TSU I took with me to U of H. and not attending classes was one of them, I fell behind and eventually I was suspended, I was devastated. I was never in class; I was traveling around the Nation with my Pastor in crusades and revivals. I was teaching street services, helping ministers plant churches, being busy and I had no idea that I was being set up for greatness even while I was being foolish, dabbling with sinful practices; GOD was still keeping me. I gained a lot of knowledge, set under some of the most prominent, influential Baptist preachers in the Nation. God blessed me and I had no idea that a day would come and I would finally realize I was set up to be great. In one arena I was succeeding and the other I was failing. My Pastor, Dr. C.A. W. Clark saw the tears in my eyes when I got the suspension notice from U of H. He told me it was time to major in what I minoring in. He was telling me my call and purpose was ministry. I could not believe that, I am Baptist and I am a Woman. Those two did not equal preacher in those days.

Greatness is in my DNA. I had no idea GOD's plan, purpose, position in life was to perfect me and prosper me. I also did not know that greatness would require so much from me. I had no idea that it would require so many sleepless nights, so much family conflict, turmoil, misunderstandings, marrying wrong men for all the wrong reasons, children out of wedlock, the loss of friends, I would eventually go through foreclosures and repossessions, business openings and closings. I went through Church establishments and Church dismantling. I would go through having to walk away from opportunities that would prosper me. I would walk away from traveling opportunities on other continents, speaking engagements, planting new Churches, excepting church assignments. I missed out on moving to different states to plant churches, accepting marriage proposals. I went through sickness, disease, dysfunctional situations, problem children and so much more. I never would have thought that I would have been unmarried and celibate for decades, not know the love of a man even in my fifties, I had no idea that I would become mega super obese, a cancer survivor, have more degrees than a thermometer. I would have never put together that my ability to bounce back from every circumstance would be part of my story. I am resilient!

I started preaching in 1992, licensed and ordained, I founded and organized a church in 2000, I was so obese by then I was sitting down preaching. I was preaching one morning about the healing power of Jesus and I heard the Lord say, nobody will believe you because you need healing yourself. That was my eye opener! I went on a journey to find better health. I lost half my weight by 2006, I lost the first 168lbs in 2005, it took 8 months, and I had surgery. I was so excited that I was much more mobile. It was good for me. I lost as much as I could and then it stopped. I had so much hanging skin that it was painful to walk or exercise. I could injure myself because the skin would hit me back.

GOD fixed that! I found a plastic surgeon that could help me. That was a long journey, every time I went to be cleared for surgery, something happened, the last time was breast cancer. I had a triple negative progressively fast growing cancer in my right breast. It was found by accident while trying to get the fat and skin removed from my belly. I thank God because it had only been 3 months since my last CT scan and it was not there. It was growing so fast that if I had waited to have surgery or if it had not been found then, I would not be here to write these few pages. I was kissing death in the forehead and God saved me!

Cancer was not in the plan; I wanted all that skin sitting in my lap off. That weight was like having a 5-year-old child sitting in your lap and you cannot get them off. Cancer trumped the stomach surgery. I was not happy. I did not go into a long spill; there were no tears. I did not get depressed and as of today I have not had the emotional shock that I was suppose to get from it. I prayed Lord this was not part of my plan, can we get this out of the way. He heard my prayer. I had the surgery, went home breast less, healed, went through chemotherapy, all of this while finishing my second Bachelors, starting a new Master's program and my grades did not suffer.

I stayed focus and I realized that cancer was a journey. I can tell you that it was an interesting journey. I was in the middle of chemotherapy, several issues happened. I lost a couple of vehicles, I was not working, I was on disability and I loss a third of my income then. So my money was funny and my change was strange. My son, my boy, my baby boy, the only boy, got in trouble and was sent to prison. It was the beginning of his awakening, his journey to find out his potential, and his greatness. My son, my help was gone. Lord what am I going to do without Christopher? His girlfriend brings his vehicle to me to keep, well thank you God for transportation, I would rather have my baby.

I am in chemo, my kid would see about the hard stuff, the picking up heavy stuff, etc. My daughter had her hands full with pre-teens and a teenager. She really did not have the time or the know how to deal with me. She would come to my rescue when I had sense enough to articulate how much I needed help. My son and I think alike, he knew me. He would have had things done before I could even tell him what to do. I sucked it up because I knew "I was created to get this done".

I honestly felt alone, I had a gazillion friends and church members but I was alone. People felt sorry for me at least for a little while until they saw I refused to die. It was lip service though, no one ever thought about the things I was not able to do, the simple things like sweeping, mopping, cleaning. I really hated the thought of somebody feeling sorry for me. I hated more that nobody thought about how much time I spent alone and how I could have used some help. I suppose they did not know how to help me and I did not know how to ask them or teach them. I have always been the giver not the receiver. It was awkward needing help! I just got things done. I was creative.

God gave me a new crew who knew how to support me. I befriended a gentleman on social media, we had so much in common academically and we would spend hours on line both of us studying and reading, we would look up from our computers every now and then and smile, have an intellectual conversation and go over what we had learned. We had a wonderful relationship. We met before I was diagnosed and had time to spend together; him teaching me about his love for golf, taking me to see beautiful golf courses in his hometown. He walked with me through the cancer and the chemo. He thought I was the strongest person in the world because I was strategic in my plan and my prayers. I walked through his sports season with his children playing sports, listening to him talk about the adventures of having a senior citizen and a child going through puberty in the house at the same time. We kept each other going. Little did I know eventually I would be in the same situation with a child going through puberty and a senior citizen in the same house, he prepared me for it.

He knew when my chemo was rough; he knew how to comfort me. He was very supportive and I thank GOD for the time I had to spend with him. It was in the middle of this journey, this walk through cancer that my friend had a conversation one Thursday morning with me. He told me he had a project do for class and he and his classmate were go-ing to the clinic to film their portion of the project and he would check back with me after my visit. I will make this brief. He made a comment to me that was very kind, I told him, "I love you for that".

I did not know that would be the last time I would hear his voice. That morning he had a massive heart attack, major surgery that re-sulted in him having a massive stroke and by Monday he was brain dead. I felt like I finally knew what it was like to suffer great loss. Sure I have suffered many deaths, grandparents, my adopted mother, friends, sister and brother (my natural siblings) yes I have met with death on many occasions, as a sister, child, grandchild, cousin, friend, wife, preacher and pastor; but this time and one other time the sting of death wounded me for a moment. I really had to shake myself. I was grateful that I had a group of online preacher friends that supported me through laughter. I tell you the ability to laugh saved me; it was the only medicine for me I had to laugh through grief, sickness and finan-cial ruin. I encourage people to find something to laugh at. I realized that the goal was to conquer cancer, chemo and chaos. I am resilient and that is phenomenal!

After my friend left me, I drowned myself in my studies, I finished my chemo and 2 weeks later in my second term of my Master's program I went to my ceremony for my Bachelors degree. I was grateful to make it to Miami. I was broke and I could not afford to go but I bought my cap and gown as an act of faith. I made it. I went by bus but I made it. Being there with tens of thousands of graduates old and young, handi-capped and not, I got to see many people dealing with adversity that understood their plight. It gave me much hope. I could keep going! I finished the Master's program and like the first time I bought my cap and gown believing I would make it to the ceremony. I did not, I trusted in someone else and they let me down. I was angry at myself because generally I have a plan, I did not this time. I was hurt but knew regardless of the ceremony I had the degree; it was in my hand along with the transcript so nothing else really mattered. I got over myself and enrolled in the doctorate program. This was awesome moment in my life!

I had an earned doctorate degree but I never used the title. This one was on a different level and I felt like the work I put in will feel more like I earned this one. I did well in the program, had a few obstacles; I left my home to move in with my dad right before my classes started. I had no idea the plight of my father but he was diagnosed with dementia, a few other issues and to top all that off; I observed he was bi-polar. Trust me an elderly person that is bi polar and has dementia is a ticking time bomb, scary at best. This made me understand my childhood; both my parents we weird but they balanced each other out and worked well together, I think that is what masked the issue.

Living at my dad's house made it hard to work. It was hard to focus. My health was failing and I was miserable, this was not my environment, not my atmosphere but he needed me. By the time I got settled and now on medication, my doctor telling me I am going to stroke out if I don't figure things out. I am going through all this and my father tells me to get out. Devastated and angry, I spent all I had to move in, spent my last to get him straight, and lost my at-home job because of his shenanigans. He wants me out! Well I moved and vowed never to come back. I left, stayed with my natural mother 3 weeks and her house had become chaotic, I could not stay there so I went to my daughter's for less than 3 months. I found a nice place to stay and once again I have my atmosphere. 5 months after that, I am driving home and the Lord brings my dad up. I go by there and things are not good. He is sitting in a bad place and I knew if I did not rescue him; Adult protective services would. I started back seeing about him until I went by one day fed him gave him food for the weekend. All he had to do was microwave it. I went back that Monday and realize he had not eaten since Thursday. I knew he did not need to be alone. Once again I am faced with moving in with him. Here we go again. It was a bit different this time. It was harder in some ways, easier in others. I was still frustrated, still angry that this falls on me. This is not my blood but I am stuck here. Nobody else is coming to rescue him. I am trying to look at this in a different light. I still asked GOD why? I promised him I would not put him in a facility unless I could not protect him. I still wondered why everybody else (my siblings and his relatives) get to enjoy life. They get to enjoy being married having partners, being with their families building their dreams. Why do I not get the opportunity? If I am stuck here I cannot really date. I have all kinds of crazy thoughts going through my mind. I finally had to say to myself enough is enough. One thing at a time lets finish school, let's get this out of the way. Then we can revisit these thoughts. I moved on, thoughts can overwhelm you! I had to focus!

Funny, I learned so much about myself that I never ever thought about. I always knew I was a pretty good student. My grades were pretty good. I knew that but what I did not know was that I was more than a good student. I was exceptional-I was a high achiever. My understanding was excellent; I had to learn that I was a scholar.

Three almost four years later I am at the end of my PhD program in Advance Studies of Human Behavior. I am becoming Dr. Dianne, for the second time. I also have 3 honorary doctorate degrees. So cancer was over, chemo over but the aftermath of chemo still exists. Chemo left me with a few health problems, I manage not to let it get me down, but I suffer. I have issues; things are not perfect in my life. I can probably whine and complain about at least 50 things but there is no use. I have the answer to every problem I have. I have the ability to be who I want to be, create what I want to create, explore what I want to explore. I have the ability to bless GOD's people, with wisdom and knowledge because He has paved the way for me. I told you there was a purpose for me coming out feet first. I have to walk it out.

I did not detail all the issues that I have had in my life because there are so many people that have suffered more than me. I can say I have had the most bizarre things to happen. I have made some of the craziest decisions that anyone could make. I have paid handsomely for my stupidity. Regardless of the mistakes I have made like a good Father, God has always forgiven me, chastised me when I needed it, showed me my errors, showed me where I needed to change or which turn I needed to make. What I can say is be encouraged, stay on the path. I have learned that the path you are on is where the doors you want opened should be opened. Many times we are on a path but try to open doors not on the path. Stay on the path, watch what God hands you, doors begin to open, things begin to happen and success comes.

I am a phenomenal woman, not because of my brilliance, not because of my beauty but because of my beliefs. It is my belief in GOD, my belief in His plan for my life that has placed me in a position to be an extraordinary woman. Every success is because of GOD. My life has not been easy; it has been difficult. I have given up much for others and sometimes the ground I sowed in was not good ground, so there was no harvest other than the harvest of a bad experience, which is a lesson learned. I am still struggling with the journey, currently taking care of an aging parent with dementia, but GOD has graced me to finish school, teach his people and take care of my father. I am resilient because I can thrive in chaos. What I do know is it will not always be a struggle; all is well because I am a phenomenal woman. YES that is me!

CHAPTER 8

THE TURNING POINT

Teresa Beene

Now Faith is the substance of things hope for, the
evidence of things we don't see."

HEB 11:1

"So AFTER YOU have suffered a little while, He will restore, support and strengthen you, and He will place you on a firm foundation" I think Peter really knew what he was talking about when he wrote this scripture.

Suffering is an interesting word. I hear people use it so much in this day and time. People suffer from a headache, suffer from and illness, they suffer because they don't have a cell phone or it is broken, the cable goes out or they have to do without having their favorite coffee or favorite bottled water. Any time a person denies themselves of something they love; nowadays it is referred to as suffering. This is what we call suffering. If we only understood real suffering we would be more compassionate, more concerned and more forgiving of others and things.

Many people would say I suffered much in my young years, I did not know it was suffering; I thought it was just living. I think GOD has a way of shielding you from things while you are in the midst of them. What makes me a phenomenal woman is my ability to adapt, to evolve to learn from my experiences. I am agile, resilient and able to bounce back. My experiences would make some people throw in the towel, tap out, wave the flag, just plain old quit! I have endured much turmoil, much poverty, much hurt and pain, death, sickness, even some embarrassment, but the love I received helped me endure, blinded me from knowing that my situation was considered bleak. If it was not for love and its enduring factors, I would have never been strong enough to get to where I am today. I would have never made the decisions that got me to my right now! I would have never experienced my turning point! My turning point certainly led me to being the Phenomenal Woman that I am. Yes indeed! I am still standing.

I was born in Haynesville, Louisiana-A very small town where everybody knew what was going on in town. I was born to a very young mother, she was only a girl just beginning adolescence, looking to find herself; she was only 14. My father was 10 years her elder. In some cultures this still ok, but many have gone to prison or jail. She was a minor.

My mother lived with her mother and father and the house was a small shotgun house. We were piled in the house like sardines in a can.

The living room, I guess we would call it the front room was full of beds, bunk beds and full size bed. There were at least 10 of us at a time. My grandparents, some of their children, and their children's children; it was a busy household. My grandfather was the sole financial support for the house. He worked; my grandmother took care of the house and the children. My parents never married, but my family was an interesting one. My mother and her brother were dating my father and his sister. My parents did not marry but my uncle on my mother' side did marry my aunt on my father's side. The easiest way to say it, to explain it; we were complicated kinfolk!

My mother had 2 other children by the time she was 20. So much was going on at the time. It was always a lot of people living in that small house. My grandmother was just that caring. I knew things were not the same as other children that I met or knew but I never heard the words, we are too poor, there was always a solution to every problem I encountered, my grandmother made sure of that. She always provided what she could.

At a young age I had several experiences that I really did not understand. I did not have a close relationship with my father, he was visible but we were not close. My father and my mother obviously had some type of relationship; otherwise I would not be here. They were not a couple; my father decided to build a life with my mother's cousin. Like I said, we were complicated kinfolk. I knew who he was and occasionally spent time at his house on weekend trips and some days in the summer; but I often felt like he was more of a father to my half sister than he was to me. I explained that my father and my mother had siblings that married each other. My mother's brother married my father's sister. I guess my complicated kinfolk in some circles would be called "double kin". This means that I have cousins that are kin to me on my mother's side of the family and my father's side of the family. This is a hard thing to explain, to many people.

I mentioned death. My first encounter with death and I don't have all the details was with my father killing my uncle, my mother's brother. Can you imagine the turmoil behind this? For children, this is a complicated situation. You hear the chatter about who is responsible, but nobody ever sits down and explains to you what happened. I remember my Big Momma being in denial about this and teaching my brother that he was not his father for the shame I guess she felt. Big Momma raised my brother and in my opinion, she was abusive to him and to this day I believe he is haunted by childhood memories of the abuse he suffered. The flip side of that is my grandmother, who really is my parent, my most responsible parent; lost her son in all of this and still remained able to show love and support never badmouthing my father to me or calling him awful names. There must have been extenuating circumstances, because he was never imprisoned for it.

A couple years later, my mother moved out of the house and was living with her boyfriend. She would come by and take me to my doctor's appointments, do whatever was necessary for me and my siblings. My grandmother did not drive; neither did my mom have a car; which meant we walked a lot. Although my mom was not there to do all of the motherly things, she was present and she was able to help out along with my Uncle Ray. Our life was really pretty tough. When I look at it from my current status in life; when I compare where I am and where I was. I don't know how we made it through all that adversity. We did not have much; I could almost say we had nothing! We did not have nice clothes but we were dressed, we missed out on a lot of things that are necessary for success in life but we were taught how to make do. I remember a time when I was in elementary school, we did not have the luxury of notebook paper to write our homework assignments on; we wrote on whatever was available, like the paper bags from the grocery store. The point was to get the assignment done! I was taught to make the effort, no excuses. Sometimes we were the laughing stock of the school because our hair wasn't combed, maybe because my Uncle Ray didn't get a chance to come by the night before to comb it for us.

I guess I was immune to peer pressure. I did not understand that my situation was considered grim; I knew others lived better than us but I did not dwell on it. Growing up not hearing people whining about being poor or living in lack may be the reason I never really knew how bad things were.

Even in all of that poverty and adversity tragedy struck again, my grandfather and his nephew was killed in a car accident. My grandfather, the sole supporter of the house, the only crutch my grandmother had was gone. I watched her walk through this one like a champion. No money, no way to keep the lights, water, and gas on or rent paid. There was nothing and the landowner wanted his property back. He owned all the land where the little shanties' or shot gun houses were. So now we have the task of moving with no income. How do you do that?

We did it! My grandmother found a little house for us to stay in; there was no indoor plumbing in the house. NONE! We had to depend on the neighbors for water, my grandmother was productive, she warmed water for us to bathe, she washed clothes in buckets, and she made us a place to use the bathroom! She did what she needed to do for us to survive. There were times we had no food, she would send us to Miss Queen Esther's house for and egg sandwich. We had no iron or ironing board, my grandmother found and old iron that did not work; she stripped the cord from it and heated on the stove to iron our clothes. She always made sure that no matter what we had it was taken care of. We learned to live with lights on or off, water on or water off, we learned to SURVIVE.

During the course of all this survival, death met us again, my mom killed her brother. My mother was trying to break up a fight between him and his girlfriend. They were all partying; of course alcohol and drugs can be a time bomb waiting to explode. So once again another tragic event, another life lost. My grandmother has lost 2 sons one by the hands of my father, the other by the hands of my mother. Now she is burying her son, grieving his lost and visiting my mother faithfully in jail.

We lived in a small town where everybody knew your business, I was excused from school to attend the court proceedings, each day until it ended I went to the courts with my grandmother and daily I had to walk this long haul way, it seemed like miles it was so long to me. They would take me to my mother to spend time with her. I was in the 2nd grade at that time. My mother was given a 7-year sentence where she served two years. She was sentenced to a prison in South Louisiana. I was afraid of her. When she came home I would run from her I was so scared to be in the same room with her. I probably felt more fear of my mother's presence than any other tragic event. Eventually she and her boyfriend, James Logan moved to Eldorado Arkansas. My Mother is an alcoholic and alcohol has ruined her life. These are the demons that tend to snuff out the life of people who have purpose and never find that purpose, never walk out their destiny because they allow the taste of temptation call them to a place that sometimes seem to have no return.

By the time we got a good pattern of living going on, the city condemned the house. We had to move again. At this time in my life, my grandmother was getting older; as she struggled to keep things together she depended on the assistance of my Aunt Peggy and family friend, Demetris to help us to get our baths and be fed. My grandmother also depended a lot on my Uncle Ray.

There was a small trailer on Smitherman Street. My grandmother found work. She worked for a lady, Mrs. Rogers was her name, and she paid her twice a week to clean her house. She made fifty dollars per week and the woman gave her a lot of groceries, so we had food. My grandmother managed to save a little money and get a bank loan to buy the trailer. It was not a great place but it was more than we had and she made it work for us. She still took care of me, my siblings were with others and she had my aunts 2 children, my aunt was disabled. Things were getting a bit better...there was some stability. We had food, we had a roof and we had indoor plumbing once again!

Two years past and our trailer burned! Once again we experienced a great loss! Imagine losing a son, your husband, a nephew, your home, another place and now you have gotten through all of that to lose another home. Fortunately there was insurance on the trailer and my grandmother was able to buy house on Marietta Street, a little larger a 3 bedroom one bathroom house. During this time it was my grand-mother, my two cousins and I living there. My grandmother's health was on the continued decline so my mother came back to help out. She lived in the apartment building behind our house. My grandmother still had siblings but they did not live close, only one lived near, Aunt Jenny she was a widow and never had any children; my grandmother suffered great loss, husband, children and grandchildren.

By this time my grandmother was receiving survivor benefits from my grandfather's social security so this helped her pay the bills, during this time she was ill so she depended on my uncle to pay the bills. There were times I would come home and there were no utilities. I guess the money was coming in but the bills were left unpaid. I did not receive child support; my cousin, whom we called, Dime would help get things for me. It was hard to watch my half sister be provided for after all we had the same dad, and her mother was my natural cousin. It was not something you dwell on but as a child, you just wonder why!

By the time I was in the 10th grade I was pregnant and miscarried, I repeated that same behavior again and lost that child as well. By the time I was a senior my grandmother was wheel chair bound. My grand-mother was not able to make it to my graduation or my father but my mother was there. I graduated that May and was in the Military by July. I had my basic training in Ft Jackson South Carolina, then on to Ft Lee Virginia. I would ultimately be headed back to be stationed in Louisiana. Three months into my military career my grandmother passed away. I did not get to say good-bye to her before I left for basic training. I would see her before I left each day. Things were moving too fast that day, it was time for me to go and I did not get to tell her I was leaving. While she was ill, I received a call that she was in hospice and I was able to go home to see here. I went back to my station and it was not long before my grandmother passed away.

I had experience much death in my life, I believe I took her passing well but it was a little different that the others because she had always been there for me.

During my military tour, I got pregnant. I did some sleeping around while in the military. I had the daddy issues, I believe. I was looking for love in all the wrong places, not finding love but finding situations and circumstances. Now I have a new one, a new situation. I had been dating this guy. I was pregnant. I had some real serious health issues with the pregnancy. My blood pressure went untreated and I had a blood disorder. I left short of my 4yr term some weeks, because of my health. I was on my way to the doctor's office because of the blood pressure I stopped to visit my mom and ended up missing my appointment. I went home and I began to feel really bad, I felt so bad all I could do was call for the neighbor who in turn called my uncle to pick me up and take me to the hospital. They had a very hard time managing my blood pressure; my blood pressure could rise to numbers like 270/150. I got to the hospital and I was told my baby was dead. I was 9 months pregnant, a full term baby. The hard and strange thing is you are told that you are carrying a dead baby inside of you and now you have to go to a hospital in Shreveport, Louisiana to birth the child. At that time they never told me what happened, it could have been anything, it mimicked the signs of toxemia but it was not diagnosed. I have a baby that is lying in my womb with no life.

I cannot really say I grieved but I think this one was a little more to think about than even my grandmother. I think this one was closer to me; this is a real baby that had to be born, named and buried. This was a little girl that was fully developed I have now got to put to rest. I never had the chance to see her smile or cry. I had to bury her. I pushed my way through this too. My father and stepmother did make the funeral arrangements along with myself; Kiona's father paid for the services and we had a graveside service for my little baby Kiona.

After the burial of Kiona, the one thing I knew, the one thing I was sure of was I no longer wanted to live in that town. One-day opportunity presented itself, my friend, half sister and I decided to move to Dallas, Texas. We had nothing but fifty dollars between the three of us. My half sister had a brother in Dallas and we stayed with him in a one-bedroom apartment. It was hard! We were young, dumb and trying to make it. My friend and my half sister went home; I stayed. I had another cousin and I moved in with her.

It is hard staying with other people especially when you don't have a job; I felt alone. My cousin did not know me so we had no relationship; my sister and friend were gone. I felt alone. My cousin had a cousin. I started dating him. He was in an 8-year relationship with his child's mother. His family was not happy with his decision to break off the relationship. There were times I did not eat because I had nothing; I would see him on weekends. He was the one who helped me. He was my friend. Fortunately for me I was able to find a job as a detention office for the Sheriff's office. I got an apartment and Aric moved in; we got married and 3 months after we married I left and went back home. He followed me. His family was not happy, my family was not happy. It was like it was their marriage and not ours. He decided to go home and I followed him. This was hard and awkward. I did not have a job because I quit to go home; he does not have a job because he quit to follow me. So we are totally dependent on his family for everything. I joined his church; we counseled with Pastor Johnson, we were determined to push through; the odds were stacked against us. I felt alienated-not a part of the family.

Things began to changed I got a job at Braum's went to Medical Assistant school at Ultrasound Diagnostics. I then was blessed with a full time job at a Charter school. I worked days, went to school at night. I was pregnant! This pregnancy was very hard. I had a good team of doctors that got my medical records and looked at my history of pregnancies and how they all were unsuccessful. They monitored me very carefully because of my history. I had my baby boy! Christian. It was not 24 hours later that my child was in critical condition. He had turned gray, he had stopped breathing and was seizing. They worked on him and told me that his head was full of blood and the opening in his cavity that was to drain was very small. He would not last 24 hours and they moved him to the Neonatal care unit at Methodist Hospital. Here I am in the hospital less than a day from delivering him and they are moving him. I have to follow my son. I wanted to be discharged and they said NO. I had the same blood disorder, this was the culprit, and this was the reason that the others did not make it. Protein S in a blood clotting disorder that can cause blood clots that can be deadly. It is far worse in infants because the clot can be anywhere in the infants body. In this case the blood was in his head. There was no way I could stay there for treatment. I had to see about my son, I did not have time for treatment. I told them I would see a doctor about the blood thinners. I left the hospital!

I saw the pediatric neurologist who explained the problem in more detail. The news was horrific; the doctor says IF he survives he will have brain damage. The odds are against us. They do not expect him to live but if he does, he will have brain damage! What parent wants to hear this news? We broke down right there in the waiting room my husband and me. I had finally heard the worst of the worst news. This was the one that made me know grief. My prayer was Lord don't let my baby suffer, if he is going to die then take him now! My in-laws were there-I now have tears. I cried a lot, trying to wrap my mind around the crisis. That moment was the turning point in my life; it was the turning point in the life of my husband. This situation changed us both; it brought awareness to us like we had never had before. God truly had our attention. For 13 days we were in waiting mode, the blood had finally filtered. We received a call asking if we wanted to spend the night at the hospital. They told us this would be a good idea so we could learn how to care for our son so we could take him home! GOD not only turned us but He turned the situation around. It was indeed a miracle!

We were told that my son would have brain damage, and then we were told he had a mild case of autism. Christian is a 9th grade student attending regular classes. He has asthma and a few allergies but there are no other health issues. My husband was delivered that very night from wanting to run the street and drink. He had no classes, no meetings, and no counseling! God changed him that night and he has been home, working, taking care of, and spending time with his family for the last 14 years. 2 years later Xavier was born.

I have still had some health issues my blood pressure still would get out of control my blood sugar would spiked to 500 and even 1000. It took a year to regulate my levels. We were in San Antonio and I lost all control of my body functions. I was very ill. I had to have my gall bladder removed. I never mentioned to them about the blood disorder. It slipped my mind because I was not having any problems. I was not being treated for it. A week later I had 4 blood clots in my lungs, it took them 8 hours before they knew what was wrong. I could not get my breath and my husband would stand me up so I could catch my breath. A nurse came in and raise my shirt, asked me had I had a recent surgery, I said yes. She knew that I had blood clots. Six months later I had a hysterectomy. I claimed my healing. In 2014 I was healed!

I have endured many trials and tribulations. Like Paul says I know how to be abased and I know how to abound. In order words I know how to appreciate very little and I know how to appreciate much. I believe GOD allowed all of this to keep me balanced and leveled for the continued journey ahead. There is much to live for. I am a walking, talking, breathing, living testimony. I have lost much but I have gained more. I thank GOD for my Turning Point because my Turning Point is what made me into the Phenomenal Woman that I am and Yes! I am still standing!

CHAPTER 9

DIVINELY RESTORED

Jennifer Nash

"Destiny is not a matter of chance, but a matter of choice. It's not a thing to be waited for; it is a thing to be achieved."

–WILLIAM JENNINGS BRYAN

LIFE HAS THE ability to surprise you and take you through all kinds of turmoil, especially when the enemy is involved. You see this serpent had it in for me since conception; he was all in my business. This dirt devil tried all throughout my life to take me out every chance he got. I went through life being motherless, living with a grandma who didn't like me much, losing loved ones, being called ugly and too dark, sharing my man (husband) with every woman that lived in Chicago, homelessness with my children to everything else that was imaginable. I felt that I was cheated out of life. I knew that somehow and someway I had to keep moving, keep pressing, and keep persevering while I was riding the storms of life. I had to keep holding on to God's unchanging hands, no matter how bad I wanted to let go of everything because of all that was going on around me. The enemy was so deep on my track it felt like I was in hell's stomach. I couldn't see or feel my way out. It felt like war and the devil was winning. He tried to kill me off slowly but surely. The devil tried to take me on a road trip to damnation but didn't know that Jesus was my DRIVER. As those remnants of my past begin to play in my mind, I begin to wipe the tears as they fell from my face. It was at that moment that I realized that the Lord was restoring my soul! The Psalms rings so clearly in my mind! HE RESTORES MY SOUL!

I know I'm Phenomenal; the enemy has been at me since birth. I was the product of a 15 year old; born weighing two pounds and fourteen ounces; premature with the odds against me. No neonatal or preemie centers, no state of the art technology but I stayed in the hospital for a couple of months until I reach the size of a healthy baby. I MADE IT! The devil thought that he was going to take me out, but God turned that situation around.

I was divinely destined to survive it all! Only when my life began to fall into divine alignment with the Word and God's will, did restoration begin! Who knew in spite of my background and how I grew up, that God would have even thought of, looked at or smiled down on me? He has a plan and a purpose for each one of us, through the good, the bad, and the ugliest situation ever imaginable.

A MOTHERLESS CHILD

Growing up in a place without my mom was heartbreaking at times and it took a toll on my life. My mom gave me up when I was 9 years old to my father's side of the family in Milwaukee, WI. I did not know them very well. She knew she could not take care of us. She was tired of battling with everything and she felt it was best for us. My mom was in an abusive relationship with my stepfather and was on all types of drugs and alcohol. We would watch my mom go in and out of rehab every 2 to 3 months only to end up the same way. They would always fight; he would beat her so bad that she would be afraid for us. At times we would help her fight him back; he would hit us too. It was like going through a revolving door that never stopped.

I knew who God was at the young age of 7 because my neighbor took us to church with her. I loved VBS (vacation bible school) and youth night because it made us feel important we could forget about our problems. It was my brother, my sister and I. I was the oldest my brother was behind me a year, my sister 2 years. My mom never took us to church nor did she ever go with us when we invited her. I knew it was the drugs they kept her away. I prayed for God to fix my family because I knew we were broken. I know now that God had His hand on my life.

One horrible moment in my childhood was at age 6. The gas was off the house was cold and we were forced to sleep in my stepfather's friend room; it was warm. His friend was not supposed to be there. I woke up to find him between my legs, I tried to scream for help but he covered my mouth with his huge hands. I passed out from shock of what happened. My mom woke me up the next morning he was on the couch. I started crying because he was looking at me while my mom changed my clothes in front of him and she hollered at me for it. When I came home from school I tried to tell my mom but she brushed it off. She told me I was lying and to sit down. I told my stepfather and he had a fight with him and put him out. I wanted to go to my real father's house so bad and tell him what happened. I no longer felt safe there. My mom said no, because she already knew what was going to happen if he knew. I told my grandparents but they were battling their alcohol demons. My father passed away about 4 months later and I really felt alone and like a motherless and a fatherless child; hopeless as well with no one.

My mom kept us until I was 9, she took us to Wisconsin and my aunt took custody of us. We became wards of the state. There were 7 children living there who included my siblings and me. I was 14 when we ran away from the abuse from my aunt. We went to my mom's, she was living in Milwaukee, and we told her about the abuse, showed her the bruises from the beatings we had the previous night. She called the police and they came out to take pictures and ask questions. Since we were wards of the state they had to call our social worker and inform her. We were only allowed to stay at my mom's that night. We were taken from my mom and could not be around her unsupervised. I really wanted my mom and I missed her so much.

My sister and I went to a foster home and two group homes within 4-6 months. My grandma was in custody court fighting to get us. I was a mom to my little sister and did not want to be divided from her while we were in and out of the system. My grandma finally gained custody; we went back home in Chicago in July 1992. My brother wanted to go back to my aunt's but eventually ended up with us months later.

WHILE RIDING THROUGH THE STORM

From age 14 to18 I thought things were stable but it turned bad. My grandma was an alcoholic; she took custody of us only for the money. She favored my sister over me and compared our looks and our father's background. Yes my sister was light skinned with pretty hair and I'm chocolate with a nice grade of hair. I was the black sheep of the family. The devil was still trying to take me out but God had his hands on me. I was the oldest but I was mistreated, my sister and I were not treated the same. I was not allowed to use the washer or cook food even though she was getting food stamps and money for us. My grandma started cursing me out, accusing me of things. She acted as if she hated me.

I went to church when we moved back to Chicago with my childhood neighbors. I knew about spiritual things at a young age. The more I went to church the more the enemy attacked me through my grandma. My sister and I were close, nothing could break our bond, and she did not like how my granny treated me. I begin to see evil spirits on my grandma and her face took on different forms. My grandfather helped to take care of us because my grandma abused our money and gave our food stamps to her friends.

I had my first boyfriend at the age of 14 and I was pregnant by age of 16. His grandma stayed across the streets from us. They were my second family before I became involved with him. I grew up with the whole family. While I was pregnant with my first child, I was hungry and my grandma would starve me. She denied me food and the use of the kitchen until my granddad got on her. Thank God for WIC and my in laws because that's how I ate. My granddad looked out for me when I was home, my sister would help also. My grandma also pulled my granddad's army rifle on me; she also hit me with a broom in the stomach when I was 7 months pregnant. She would always belittle me; call me names, telling me I was going to be like my mom. I endured some pretty horrible things from her.

I gave birth to my daughter on May 25, 1995 at the age of 17. That was the most precious day of my life because I had my own child to love and she could love me back. My sister was so happy that she had a niece. She was born 4 days before her 15th birthday. I wished I had my mom in my life at that time. I was feeling like I really needed her especially since I had just given birth to my baby. 5 months after giving birth, another tragedy happened in my life.

Tragedy seemed to be the "normal" in my life. My sister was killed. She was an innocent bystander during a drive-by shooting across the street from our house. She was on her way home from the store from getting my granddad some medicine. She was walking with her friend; the same bullet that shot my sister grazed our friend under her breast. I was in the house asleep with my baby but I seemed to jump straight up from my sleep. I felt like something was terribly wrong. The neighbors came running upstairs yelling for us to call the police and ambulance because my sister had been shot. I jumped to the floor and ran down the stairs while putting on my skirt. When I got across the street to my sister; she was barely conscious and I put my fingers in her hands and told her to respond by squeezing my hands. She squeezed my hands for the last time and let go. I passed out for about fifteen minutes before my family and friends got me to fresh air, I knew she was deceased. Growing up on the south side of Chicago at that time was like being in a hellhole; there was always a death threat! It was all about survival!

I took it pretty hard for a while. I began to question God about taking my best friend from me. I felt there was a void in my soul. Months later I moved into my very own apartment. It was a month before my 18th birthday because I couldn't stand to live in that house without my sister. It did not seem real to me...she was gone!

I was 19 when I married my childhood sweetheart, February 1997 and I was the happiest person that day! It was one of the best moments of my life; I was told it was the Godly thing to, do since we were shacking. I had a few good moments in between my bad moments! Things seemed to be going really good, I had accepted Jesus into my life a month after we were married. He was in the music ministry and I was in the choir. The enemy did not like what we were doing or what we were going to become in the Lord; so he stepped up his game plan.

I was 20 when I became pregnant with my second child. I miscarried, that was the most painful thing. 6 months later, I was pregnant again. Right before I gave birth to my son; our marriage was under attack the enemy used my husband. His game plan was in action. The only man I had ever loved; moved out a week after I gave birth; he was cheating, he had children outside our marriage. It was at that time the physical, mental and emotional abuse began. I was getting into it with the other women disrespecting me. I would say ungodly things to them in self-defense and he upheld them and edged them on. I was not moved by them, I stood my ground. Oh yeah the devil used him big time! He would bring them and their children to our church. I started feeling out of place at my own church. We were still married and he would bring his other two families to the family functions while I sat there and looked like a complete fool; at that moment I had to do something different.

I gave birth to my third child at 23; we were working on our marriage, I thought. In the middle of my 7th month of pregnancy, two other women were also pregnant. I was heartbroken and mad as Hell! The abuse would happen when he came over to see the kids. He would be mad at the other women and find reasons to take it out on me. I would argue with him about stupid things that he was accusing me of. He argues with me and has two other families? Really! One time he put his hands on me while I was in the Pastor's office making programs; he came in with the kids and started an argument about a bus card. It really was more personal than that because I was I had begun to distance myself; I was not all over him anymore. I was ignoring his comments when he came behind me and choked me unconscious in front of my babies, and this was in the church. All I can remember hearing is his little brother telling him to let me go and my kids crying. When I came to, the Pastor and First Lady had come back there and told him to leave. Instead of him leaving, I gathered my 3 children and walked out the church while it was snowing, people were calling me back. I could not go back.

I had no place to go and I knew I could not go back; I was a tired soul. It was our first night in a shelter. My children and I were in and out of family and domestic violence shelters. My husband followed us from different places back to the shelter; we were always moving. He was violent; I had to get an order of protection. I remember one night while in a shelter, the Lord woke me up and told me, "To Whom Much Is Given Much Is Required", and from that moment on I knew that the Lord was keeping us. Some days my babies and I would be hungry after leaving the shelter for the day. Most of the time we had no money; God's favor was on my life because he always made a way for us. There were times we slept at the police station and outside because the shelters were full. I could not believe we were homeless and God let us become that way. I was really mad at God.

I could not keep a job because of my husband's harassment. He really worked hard to make my life a living hell. He called child protective services on me a few times only to look foolish, because I took good care of my children regardless of where we were. The new church that I joined really looked out for my kids and me; the Lord had given us favor with them, especially the pastor.

My divorce was final April 2003. It felt like I was in the pit of hell. God had released me spiritually and physically from it. The devil did not stop there; I went through so much more with him, he did not want to help with our kids. In 2007 the Lord had spoken to me and told me to leave Chicago and go to Texas. I had just started working my second job and just moved into my new apartment. My family was getting adjusted to life and doing my home ministry that the Lord had birthed through me. I was serving at my church and the children also.

I was obedient to the voice of the Lord, I move to Dallas, Texas in October 2007 with nothing but my children and our clothes. I gave away all my furnishings. I was set up to be a blessing to someone else. I knew in my spirit I was directed to move, but in my flesh I was going to be alone. The day came when we boarded the greyhound bus headed to Dallas; I cried 10 of the 22 hours I was on the bus. The Lord reassured me that where He guides, He provides and that He would take care of my babies and me.

WHAT ABOUT THE CHILDREN?

During the times of my tests and trials I kept my children with me and didn't want to be apart from them. They went through things that they didn't see their friends go through. The years of being homeless, they suffered a great deal but they also knew that the Lord was on our side. One thing that I did was stayed in the house of the Lord with my children. I stayed involved with the different ministries and made sure that the children did too. The only thing that kept us in our right minds was Jesus. My children never went without the things that they needed. They did go through some minor things during our divorce but the Lord sustained us all.

They never failed a school grade; they stayed on top of their work. The school was also aware of our situation and provided different resources as well as counseling. One of my sons had begun to act out. There were times when they wanted to be around their dad but he wasn't always available. Through it all, we've learned to trust in Jesus all the way. Sometimes it seemed as if we were alone in our situation. We found ourselves frustrated because we lived in shelters and could not always participate in church activities and other events because of time restrictions and rules. This was heartbreaking at times. My children didn't like a lot of the shelters because some were not kid friendly. It was the best we could do at the time. The Lord was always with my children regardless of circumstances. The Lord had given my children favor, peace and love during these times. He has also blessed us with good health as well.

It is God's will for our children to be blessed of Him. Psalms 127:3 tells us that "Children are a heritage of the Lord: and the fruit of the womb is His reward". Matthew 19:14 let us know "but Jesus said suffer not the little children, and forbid them not, to come unto me, for theirs is the kingdom of heaven". Proverbs 22:6 also states "Train up a child in the way he should go and when he is old, he will not depart from it" Matthew 18:10 "Take heed that ye despise not one of these little ones; for I say unto you, that in heaven their angels do always behold the face of my Father which is in heaven." I am truly beyond blessed to have the children that God has blessed me with, despite their differences, they are all truly blessed.

PHENOMENALLY RESTORED

Isaiah 43:18-19 "Do not remember the former things, nor the things of old. Behold, I will do a new thing, now it shall spring forth; shall you not know it."

When God commanded me like he did Abram, in Genesis 12, to leave my comfort zone, from among my friends and family, to go and live in an unfamiliar place, it was not an easy pill to swallow. He was with me every step of the way. When we pulled into the Dallas bus station, there was a difference in the atmosphere and I knew that I was home where the Lord had led me to be. Everything felt, looked and smelled different than what I was use to. I knew at that moment that my whole life was about to be different. Of course I had to go to a shelter because we had nowhere else to go but this time it was for good reasons.

What I didn't quite understand in the beginning of that chapter of my life compared to this chapter of my life is that I had to go through all of the things in my past to see the fullness of what my Father was using me for. And that was for my PURPOSE AND DESTINY that He had already predestined for me. I didn't just go through for myself, but it was for everybody that is reading my story right now, and also for God's glory. "WE OVERCAME HIM BY THE BLOOD OF THE LAMB AND THE WORDS OF OUR TESTIMONY", Revelations 12:11

I currently have a fourth child, he is two years old he is a blessing to the family. I am developing a ministry, it is registered, and I am looking for sponsors. I am on my way back to school to obtain my culinary degree. I am going to start my catering business here like I did in Chicago. I also do event planning and decorating. It seems impossible to man but with God all things are possible if you believe, and that I do.

The Lord has fully restored my life from being homeless to being in my own place and other things are falling into divine alignment for my family. I am an overcomer in every area of my life (domestic abuse, sexual abuse, mental and emotional abuse, child abuse, child molestation, homelessness, church abuse and even self abuse). I am able to stand to tell my testimony and all the goodness that comes from the Lord; who is able to restore, redeem, renew, and revitalize my life to a state of Godly restitution. There is nobody but Jesus. He said, according to Jeremiah 29:11 "For I know the thoughts that I think towards you, thoughts of peace and not of evil, to give you a future and a hope."

What makes me a PHENOMENAL WOMAN, is the God in me and allowing Him total control of my life. He has taught me to be a Woman of Excellence and a Woman of Integrity. Even while I was riding through the storm of life, and the winds begin to sway me to and fro, my soul was anchored in the Lord and I held on to ALL that I knew, some days I didn't have enough strength and my spirit was too weak to speak, I would travail and moan in the spirit. Being a prayer warrior, intercessor and heavily involved in spiritual warfare; there were times when I wanted to let go of God and give up. The Lord would not let me. The enemy's B game couldn't out beat Gods A game for my life. He was mending back the broken pieces of my life. I have had pastors and ministers who would come up and tell me that they could not handle what I had been through. When I look back over my life the, Lord constantly reminds me that He only give His hardest battles to his strongest soldiers. You see, the Lord is preparing a table right before me in the presence of all my enemies, and on my table is everything that the enemy has stolen from me with interest, everything that people has told me I couldn't do and All that the Lord has for me. I love who I am becoming in the Lord. Stay tuned, there's more to come. He's not through with me yet. I have truly been DIVINELY RESTORED by the Lord!!!

CHAPTER 10

PAIN, PRAISE AND PERSEVERANCE

Kayla Roberts

"Life isn't about finding yourself. Life is about
creating yourself."

GEORGE BERNARD SHAW

THE BIBLE TEACHES us that we move from Glory to Glory! What this means to me is our Perfect GOD is always perfecting us, taking us from one level of glory to another. To get there you have to go through a process. Trust me; I have been through the process. I have been refined! I understand going from glory to glory! Sometime the process is not a pretty one but a productive one.

If someone had told me when I was young, that trouble was coming to my door and not only would it knock but it would kick the door down and invade every space of my life, that my world would be shattered, before I reach adulthood; I would have never believed them. I would never have thought in a millions years that I would have faced the kind of adversity I have faced. I never would have thought that I would be able to go through what I have gone through and make it out of it. When I put it in perspective, I am a Phenomenal!

At an early age I had to embrace motherhood. I was 16 with nothing but a lot of confusion going on in my mind. I had no idea, which way I was going. I turned to a man to lead me and help me. When you have to constantly fight for your life; that person is not worth your time. Being so young not understanding what it meant to really be loved, you can sometimes think love is one thing when it really is not. Every fight ended with him saying I made him do it. If I would just change and do what he told me to do, he would not have to hit me. In that same breath he would also say he loved me and I was the best thing that ever happened to him. If I had a dollar for every time I heard that I would be rich. I know I did not have to take that; I left him, well at least I tried.

I was a senior in high school I moved on; at least I thought I did. I started talking to someone else, but he was still a part of my daughter's life. Right before Christmas break, a girl showed up at my locker. She approached me telling me I was still messing with her man. I said nothing, because I did not want any problems in school. I told the guy I could not talk to him; I was going to go to class. I wanted no trouble with this girl or this lying guy. As I was walking away she pushed me. I snapped! I took her head to the locker. The principle asked me was I okay I said yes, but you may need to check on her. She is the one bleeding and I started laughing. That was the beginning of a downhill spiral in my life.

I started drinking and skipping school. Later I found out that I was pregnant with my second child. I am back with my abuser, the man that was beating me making me think it was all me, my fault. Yes! I am back with him. When you are a young girl and you hear those words you began to feel like maybe it is my fault and I needed to fix myself! Now here I am back with him, not only is he physically abusing me he also is cheating on me.

I received a very disturbing phone call from a young lady saying that they had just had a baby. I did not know how to respond to that, I just dropped the phone. My thoughts were expressed inward; I am thinking to myself, what I do with two children, no job and no place to go? I stayed with him, it was not the best choice but it would keep my children and me from being alone on the streets with no shelter or food to eat. This went on for two more years; while he was still cheating!

Life is full of discoveries, it is amazing to me that I slept in the same bed with a man and really did not know who he was or what he was capable of. I slept in the same bed with a man every night and did not know he was married to another woman! How could I not know? How could I miss this? Why was this oblivious to me? This is my conclusion; when you are young, dumb and not thinking, trying to survive, trying to keep your family together, so much can happen. You miss things because you are being deceived and distracted.

My second child's godmother came over to pick her up. We were chatting about things and out of the blue she asked me a question that devastated me to my core. She asked me how I felt about my baby's daddy being married. I was shocked, numb and confused. I asked her what was she was talking about. We were still together! To my surprise, that day I learned he had been married for almost three months and he also had a son one month after our child was born. If you have never seen a love triangle, this was one. When he got home that night I tried to ask him, before I could get the words out of my mouth he slapped me and told me to stay out of his business. At the tender young age of 19, with three small children not knowing what tomorrow would hold for me; I turned to God.

Late one evening my youngest son became ill. There was no reason for it, his temperature spiked.   I called his doctor and he advised me to take him to the nearest hospital. I was scared to death not knowing what was going on. The medical staff started working on him, trying to get the fever down. They had to put the IV in his head. I am a 20 year old young mother watching my child get shots one every eight hours the other every twelve hours sometimes they occurred at the same time. Crying out one night to God; I was begging him to save my son I told him if He would heal him, I would serve Him until I die. The next day my son's fever broke, his temperature was normal. It was as if nothing had been wrong with him.

The next Sunday my friend's mother sent her to pick me up. We went with them to church; I had made God a promise. I went that Sunday, but I did not go back for about two weeks. My friend and her mother came by and told me I needed to get back to church, and soon. I told her okay and went the next Sunday. There was an older man preaching that Sunday morning. This older man preached a message "Not So Lord"; I felt that he was talking to me the whole time he preached. The next thing I knew I was standing at the altar crying out asking God to save and forgive me for all my sins and to wash me and make me clean again. I gave my life to God on that Sunday June 17, 1990. Remembering I was going to have to face this man when I got back home, I decided not to tell him; at least not until I had a plan.

The next Sunday the young man preached, "God Will Make a Way to Escape". I decided to tell him we could no longer live life like we were living. He beat me unmercifully. I was holding my son in my arms. He took him out of my arms and put him on the bed with my other children as they watched him beat me. He beat me until he decided he was done. My eyes were swollen shut, my lip was busted and my entire body was hurting from the beating that I had just taken. My children were crying,

I could not see them I could only hear them. He told me that if I tried to leave him he would kill me! I was so scared and did not leave; I stayed three more months.

There was a tent revival in town; I wanted to attend. He kept the children the first couple of nights, and then he told me I could not go. I really wanted to go, so I found someone else to keep them that day. On my way out the door, with my ride waiting, he grabbed my shirt, when I tried to get away he pushed me into a brick wall busting the top of my eye open. This was the day that I decided to leave!

Two years later I met a man that I thought would be my knight in shining armor. It turned out to be a thirteen year nightmare. I gave birth to my fourth child in December 1994. He was carried passed term, he was born with fluid on his lungs and had to go into ICU were he stayed for a week. When he was released to come home, he was on a heart monitor. This was hard for me but with God's help I was able to make it through. In December 1995 I married his father. I thought this would be my happy ever after. After one month of marriage the verbal abuse began. This went on for the next 10 years.

In June 1996 our son had his first seizure. I was at work, I was told to go to Kilgore hospital. When I arrived, I saw my husband standing outside, not knowing what was going on; I ran in the hospital to find out they were working on him. My husband told me that he lost him at home and that our nine-year-old daughter called 911 and talked to them while he did CPR on our son. After about an hour they came and told us that they had to transfer him to a different hospital for more treatment. I asked if I could see my son, they took me back to see him. There were tubes all over him and machines breathing for him; my poor little baby! They put his little body into the ambulance and we followed them to Good Shepherd Hospital in Longview and met with his doctor. I was told by the doctors they were not sure what caused him to seize but would have to watch and monitor him for a couple of days.

The next morning I got a call from my neighbor who had my other children to tell me that my daughter looked as if she had had a stroke.

She rushed my daughter to the emergency room; one in ICU and the other in the ER I felt that my life was spinning out of control. After going to many doctors and specialists we found that she had what they call a TIA or a mini stroke. By this time the devil tried to take my mind; but God said not so!

Things I thought were good until October, my mother was hospitalized with what we thought was just a cold; actually she was having a heart attack. We also learned she had brain tumors and cancer in one lung. This was hard but God pulled her through it all. I suffered a stroke at the age of twenty-eight. My husband took me to the hospital; I was not feeling well, after arriving at the hospital, he had to leave so my mother came. The doctors told me that all my organs had begun to shut down and that it was not looking good for me. The one thing I did not want, was to die in the hospital, I asked my husband to come and check me out and get me to the house of God.

Sunday arrived, I was weak, my husband and daughter had to dress me and walk me to the car. At church I was seated on the on the second row; my pastor came down and told me God was about to give me a miracle. He laid hands on me and I was slain in the spirit. It felt as if I was lying on a table of needles and I could feel the blood leaving my body. Suddenly, it felt like a wind started at my feet and slowly went up my body, once it got to my head I could see a very bright light and I could hear a small still voice say it is done all is well my child.

In January of 2001 my mother had been admitted in the hospital. I was told her cancer was back and nothing could be done to help her. I asked God to prepare me for the worse, show me what was going to happen. God he did just that! God allowed be to see how everything was going to unfold concerning my mother so that I could prepare myself. I realize you can never be prepared for the lost of a parent, but it helped me to gain strength for the rest of the family.

July 9, 2001, my sister called telling me our mother was gone. That is a day that I will never forget. Grief had now entered my life. June 30, 2003, my father died in his sleep. Within two years I had lost both parents. This was quite devastating and depressing. I was mad at everyone-I questioned God about this. Most of all I was mad at my dad because he did not tell me he was leaving me. I felt cheated and alone with no one to turn to. The grief I felt was a long grueling process both parents gone. Oh Lord what else? If that is not enough to drive a person crazy in 2004 I found emails from my husband talking with his partner about how much he enjoyed spending time with him. How much more Lord?

Almost a year later I asked my husband to leave our home; I could not live like that. I knew God was able. I also knew that he, my husband, had to want to be delivered. He would have to want to change. God will not force anything on you that you do not want. That is called free will!

I tried to take my life several times; I felt I had no reason to live. Then God said look to me. That sounded real easy but it sometimes is hard. On July 6, 2006 my divorce was final. I moved to Marshall TX, to work in the school system, to start over again. I was on a new path!

Three years after our divorce, my ex-husband was ill; not expected to live. I had forgiven him and went on with my life. I felt the need to get my son to his dad's. I decided to pack up and moved to Dallas so that my son could be with his father. God had given him another chance!

God is able to keep you. I was ready to throw in the towel many times. God had to hide me from the enemy even when that enemy was me! I could not and did not want to face life anymore. My life was filled with disasters and chaos but through it all he kept me and protected me finally isolating so I could see what I really needed. What I needed was GOD. I needed to be alone with HIM so I could know who HE really is. Many times we feel that we need other people to identify who we are; when all we really need is God.

He had to show me, me. In order for Him to get the best out of me I need to be put under the magnifying glass. I needed to be processed. We sometimes think that we have to search out the answers when the answers are right before us. Life is too short not to forgive and move forward. I learned early to forgive people even when they don't think that they have done anything wrong. I have forgiven those that abused me and mistreated me.

God had to show me how to fall in love with me. In learning how to love Him, I learned to love me. In loving me I now can love others and know when I am being loved. I know what love really is, and I also know what love is not. Loving and respecting yourself is the first step to wholeness. I am now walking in the fullness of God, fulfilling the things that He has called me to do. I am a phenomenal woman and yes I am still standing.

CHAPTER 11

LIFE UNEXPECTED

Alida Smith

"Live today like tomorrow doesn't exist."

Lɪꜰᴇ ɪs ᴀ wonderful adventure. It is so full of twist and turns, one moment you are going uphill, and a moment later it is down. My adventures in life remind me of a roller coaster ride, scary and exciting at the same time. You are brave and fearful yet afraid and out of breath at the same time. Your heart races, but you are smiling. Sometimes life can be a little more subtle than the roller coaster, I guess more like a water slide. You climb to the top and your only escape is to follow the chute and ride the water all the way through the path it takes you. No way to turn around or jump off. You could end up in a couple of spots. Where you end up depends on your craftiness, how well you can ride the wave! I have found myself on the roller coast of life and through the water rides of life. I have climbed with excitement and I have gone down with a whirl, a twirl a twist, a turn and a spiral. The great thing about it is; I lived to tell the story of my life unexpected! The crazy whirlwind of life is why I am Phenomenal because I persevered through it all!

I grew up at home with my mom and my two sisters. My mom remarried when I was eleven years old. My mom always had us involved in church. I remember my friends in church were closer to me than the kids around the neighborhood. The only friends I can remember that were allowed in our house were my church friends. I was taught to respect my elders, love God and work for what I wanted.

I wasn't exposed to some of the dysfunctions in families, such as, drugs, fights, arguments; Mom was not an abusive parent. My mother never talked to me about sex. She did tell me I had better not get pregnant when she was thinking I was or might be having sex. I learned about sex in school when they taught about the human body. The way I was raised is contradictory to the way I lived.

1989, mom remarried, my sister and I were flower girls in the wedding, not long after, we had a baby brother. We were so excited to hear of our new baby brother's arrival, it had been us girls for so long. My dad was strict and I used to hate it when he gave us whippings, it stung so badly. I remember my mom put us on punishment for six months and stuck to it; no phone, no life, nothing! How embarrassing it was to only have fun during recess at school and come home to the shame of a six-month punishment. Kids made fun of us big time for that one.

My parents were working people, but not wealthy. My sister and I wore the same size and our fights usually consisted of who would wear what and who had it out first to wear. I could not wait until I turned 16. I hurried and got a job to support my clothes and hairstyles. I worked at Braum's. It was not long before I had to quit there. The slightest scent of the place, greasy burgers and ice cream made me so sick. I was pregnant!

I was 17, with my first child. I graduated from Metro-Midtown Alternative High School. I enrolled there because I skipped classes in the "traditional high school", my girlfriend and I used to get off the bus in the morning, walk the hallways and head out the back door before the first bell rang. We would come back for lunch and leave right after; back in time to catch the bus home. In order for me to graduate on time I had to go to Metro. I liked that school; not too much going on other than education and acceleration to either graduate on time or even early.

While attending Metro I dated the guy that later became the father of my son Xavier. While pregnant, going to school I managed to still keep a leveled head. I never looked for an excuse not to go to work. My mom made us switch churches to follow my dad where he was a member. It was not like my home church. We attended because we had to. My son Zay was born October '95 and I graduated January '96, yes! I got out of school as soon as I could. I didn't like school at all.

At 19 I was a manager of a clothing store. My mom relocated the family to Texas in order to keep a position in banking. I was immediately against the idea; I did not want to move! I knew nothing about Texas it was too big for my little thinking. I knew Wichita, and my kid's daddy lived there. I could not leave him! My mom told me the only way she would leave me is if I had my own place to stay. I was like cool! Kansas was not an expensive place to live; it did not take me long to find a place. I became a woman and left my childish ways behind that day. I can honestly say having kids and the expectations that comes with motherhood prepared me for what my mom told me. Little did I know I would soon be in Texas.

I was managing a clothing store. I was fired because I allowed a friend to write a check that I knew how to approve. I let her spend $2,000 dollars. She bought clothing for all of us, including the clerk that rang her out. Not a week later the district manager came down on a surprise visit. I told her the check went through and I did not know. Scared, I told the truth and went to jail. I gave the district manager the keys to my apartment to retrieve the merchandise. This was my first time in jail and it was not like jail I would see on television. I went to court and they gave me a slap on the wrist.

"Just make sure you do not get into any further trouble for the next 3 years." The judge ruled.

I met this lady named Gail, who would babysit for me. She had a nephew who I had over to my house one night. I'm thinking me and Zay's dad were not on good terms; he barely called, some days I would see him most days I did not. He was the reason I stayed in Kansas. One night he comes over while I had company. The nephew and I are lying on the living room floor. This man comes through the window on us! It's late. I am in a daze. I did not know what to do or expect. He comes in cussing, calling me names, and talking to me as if we were a couple.

He walks by me, I am still on the floor, I am afraid of what he might do and he does it! He stomps on my head. I did not say anything. There was no need in adding gasoline to the flame. The nephew says nothing! Ok baby daddy had to go! I woke from my daze and realized I am at home; he just broke into my house. I arose from the floor, went to the kitchen got a knife and ran him out quickly. I followed him all the way to the end of the walkway. In his plea of wanting me to put the knife down he reached out to me and I sliced his hand. Things were never the same after that between us.

I left the apartment and moved into my mother's house with Gail; the same house that my mom left when she relocated to Texas. I was able to help out with the bills and rent; in return Gail watched my son.

For the most part things were good. Depression hits me; having a room-mate is not all it is cracked up to be, you deal with their drama, their mood swings, and vice versa. We never fought; she was my elder. I respected her, we were like sisters and I was the little sister. She had more experience than me she was my mama away from home.

Many times I just went with the flow. I was working 2 jobs, taking care of my mama's house sending her the rent trying to stay busy. I still found myself being depressed. I would come in from work, check on my son. I would sleep until the next day. Gail knew something was not right and called my mom, she helped me realize that I was missing my family and that it may be a good idea to move to Texas. It had been delayed long enough.

The summer of 1998, I was in Texas with my family. Mom had a new house; we were the only house on the block. I was scared of the Dallas traffic so it was good my mom lived in Duncanville, a suburb of Dallas. It was not long after arriving I found a job not five minutes from the house in a call center. I never experienced this type of work before and the pay for me was phenomenal. Little did I know that finding a place would be a little more difficult than I imagined. So now this brings me to my next child.

Bianca is the product of Mr. Miller and me. I thought this man was going to be my husband. We ended up living together a few years but Mr. Miller had a problem with keeping a job. He and I both loved to smoke weed. One income, household responsibilities and two habits to support; things got sticky on the rent among other things. We moved to North Dallas, my first apartment in Dallas. Oh baby, did I loved it; nothing like Duncanville. It was so big and beautiful to me. I found a better job near where we lived. I was working at a collection agency making a little more money plus earning commissions.

Mr. Miller and I fought a lot. This always resulted in us moving a lot, we were always having to move from place to place. We were always doing the fool. The fact he never had money to give me, but was able to do what he wanted would highly set me off. He gets fired from the apartments we are living in. We are moving again and I am pregnant. This was not a good time to be having another kid. We could barely keep up with what we already had going on. The good thing about God is He hears our cry. I do not believe in abortion, but God saw fit to allow me to miscarry. I didn't listen, a few months later I was pregnant again.

While pregnant and unable to support a household with one income and one habit since I am unable to indulge due to the pregnancy, we lost our apartment in Plano. I had to move in with my older sister; Mr. Miller moved back home with his mom where I met him. I am still pregnant!

I'm still working. If I didn't do anything else I did work. No one could ever say they had to take care of me. So BB was born August '02. Mr. Miller and I were back together. We were back in North Dallas, and the last time he and I ever would fight again. We moved into an apartment with barely any furniture, I had beds and a kitchen table for us. Mr. Miller and I got into another fight. He hit me real good; the bed in our room that I had asked several times to get put up was still left in pieces. I calmly went to the room and grabbed a piece of the bedrail and knocked his behind over the head with it. Blood was everywhere it was nothing but the grace and mercy of God that I didn't kill him. He was in shock I don't think he realized what happened but noticed the blood and beckoned me to help clean him up.

Doggone it, here we go again. Moving! We moved in the same complex with a couple and their children while staying there. They were generous enough to let us stay; we shared what we could as far as expenses. But that ride soon and very soon had to end. I left Mr. Miller for good and moved back in with my sister in Cedar Hill. This brings me to my next baby, Imani.

Mr. S. was hired by my employer. I was a supervisor so I noticed him, but I was not jeopardizing my job. One day while helping the employees Mr. S slips me a note inquiring if I had a boyfriend. No, I did not at the time but was flattered that he was really interested in me. I never dated a man 14 years older than me and at the time I was in my mid-twenties. Mr. S was a different kind of man; he was a sophisticated hustler, not one that you recognized by the way he walked, talked and carried himself. He was a hardcore thug before I met him and I know those traits carried him through the years. During the course of this development I had to fire him, I could not jeopardize my job; so it was off with Mr. S's head. Regardless he knew when I got off work, I would be over. It's one thing for a man to have your body but when he has your mind, you are then his puppet and you will do whatever he tells you. With Mr. S.; I no longer had control of Alida. I was even neglecting my three kids to spend as much time as I could with him. My sister knew I was just young and dumb. I would get off work and go to his house then come home early enough to get my kids and get ready for work.

Mr. S really had me; he made me believe that it was ok for him to have other women. I went along with it. I felt like why should I have to give this man up? He has his own place, his own money, no car but knew how to get where he wanted to get. He had a lot of children none of which lived in Texas. When he found out I was pregnant he did not want me to have the baby. My beliefs were stronger than his, but he hinted to me about getting an abortion without directly asking me to do it. I had Imani September 2005.

One night, he gets a call that someone is at his place and he needs me to drop him off. I'm pregnant and hungry, he is angry. I'll never forget it-it was Chinese food. I pulled up in front of his apartment. There was a very familiar red car in the parking lot. I called him out on it while taking a bite of my food; he turns my plate up in my face spilling it all over my car. I held my head down and began to chuckle; mad as hell. I sat up and threw my right fist; I swung and hit him dead in the mouth. Oh Lord, that really pissed him off. At the time, not knowing I chipped his tooth, he came out of that passenger seat on me and balled me up like a pregnant pretzel!

After all that foolishness, I still went upstairs cleaned myself off came back downstairs where the red car still awaited him; the lady was still inside. This man had my mind; I knew he had other women. All of his ladies knew me as his sister. Everywhere we went that is how I was introduced, he had so many women. Mr. S ended up wrecking a rental car I had in my name, chasing after a lady. He ended up going to jail and later prison where he currently resides.

Mr. G is the father of my last three boys, Mr. G Jr., Alexander and King. What a whirlwind of a life I had to endure to get 3 kids by this man. Mr. G and I met the very day; he was released from prison (I was told later). I was still involved with my prison love Mr. S. My goal was to just sleep with him because he was just getting out of jail. I am thinking he is going to have it going on in bed. That jail house rock! I never had it. So it happened! He said something to me that night that made me look at him funny. I am looking for a real companion. I told Mr. G, hey my baby daddy is in jail and I am helping him out.

Mr. G said, "well you my girl now so ain't gone be none of that."

Mr. G eventually moved in. I stopped writing and helping Mr. S. This is where the world turns for Mrs. Life Unexpected. Mr. G had my heart. Now this is where you believe abuse is love. I tried to come to terms at the end of every altercation. He is living with me, going out and not coming home. We had our first child together in August 2007; our son was less than three months old. This man would not come home. So I told him I wanted him to go, this was over the phone, too scared to say it to his face. He said he wasn't leaving without his son. I packed them both up out of anger and left everything in the living room.

He left, and when I came home, he and the stuff was gone, he went to the daycare and took my son too. Dang! What have I done? How can I fix this? I begged and begged him to tell me where they were. He would not; one night he came over my friend's house and pulled up with another lady in the back seat and my son in the car seat. He let me see the baby. I kissed him but he was not going to let me take him. I could have hurt him if I tried to take him. He introduced me to this lady like he had been with her the whole time. I tried to get him back. I thought I had him.

He has another woman; Mrs. T. they are living together but he is still sleeping with me. Neither one of us would give him up. She wasn't leaving and neither was I. Mr. G and I had Alex April 2009. We did not fight over him at all. She is ok with the pregnancy, on the outside, anyway. So life goes on. Mr. G always had a key to my place, comes and goes as he pleases always making promises he is going to leave her. I thought I had come to terms with myself and had stopped messing around with him. We had fights, arguments mostly, because his abuse was more physical than mental, I knew better.

I put him on child support, what the hell did I do that for? I was pregnant with our third son, King was born February 2011. I now have to get this child support case off of him since he does live with her and they have my kids during the week and I get them on the weekends. I tried everything, but because the children were in the system; I had to file. Mr. G was pissed, but I did not want to lose him, I mean I know he is going to leave her eventually. So I said we have to get married that is the only way. So we did! King was born February 2011, months after our courthouse wedding. All this while still living with Mrs. T.

I put so much trust in this man leaving her; at the age of 34, six kids, a marriage, nothing to show for it other than my Suzuki and the fact that I am not in an insane asylum; I get to go to jail on aggravated assault with a deadly weapon charge. I found out that Mr. G was lying to me. I expected him to come and see me that dreadful night. He never showed!

I found a hammer. I drove to his house unsure if he was there or not and what would I do if he was. I called him on my way there but did not get him on the phone. I pulled my jeep up to his house, curbside. I gently got out walked up to the house. Things were pitch black and I walked up to each window facing the street and broke each one; top and bottom with the hammer I took from my house. I walked back to the jeep and drove off, looked to my left and noticed some neighbors watching the whole time. I am thinking to myself; "Noisy neighbors!" and rolled my eyes at them like, yeah I did it.

I drive back home and get in the bed. It was not long after Mr. G is calling me very upset about the windows. That same night, he and I were on the phone I asked him if she was there and he told me she was not. I knew he was lying-I was going to explode. I told him I was coming over there so we could talk. Truth was I was going to get him for all of the lies. I called my best friend; I told her I was going to jail. I knew it. She tried talking me out of it, she tried to get me to just leave the window situation at that and just go back to bed and let things die down. No, I did not do that. Still full of rage, I would not even listen to my own son; he even tried to get me to stay. I kept going.

On my way I even called my mama, she tried to calm me down;

"This is a trap, Alida. The devil is trying to destroy you," she said

I told her I was going to jail! When I saw him I was going to end it. I was going to hit him with my car; this is racing in my mind the entire ride. I am so spun out of control. I don't know if I am speeding or not. When I arrive at his home there were people everywhere. I get close enough to the house and notice Mrs. T. standing in the street next to an unfamiliar car. So many things went through my mind. I wanted Mr. G., but my actions lead me to almost run over Mrs. T.

Not long after, I hit the gas and almost smashed her between my SUV and the vehicle she was standing next to. She did feel an impact of my car, but the other car kept her from being run over. Oh Lord, I looked to my left, through all of this turmoil, and realized the Dallas police have their guns pointing at me demanding me to get out of the car. I raised my hands to surrender. They slung me out of the jeep and pinned me down to the ground. I look up and see Mrs. T is going to my jeep to get the kids while the officer cursed at me, letting me know how stupid I was for this. I did not even see them; they watched the entire thing. I was booked in the early morning of July 12th.

I had so much going on; Mr. S had wrote the courts and ended up having my three older children taken away from me by Child Protective Service. I was trying to get in touch with them before I went to jail but didn't follow up very well for this to happen. They were with my family. Forty days later…look at God; I was released on being sentenced with 8 years deferred adjudication probation for an assault against Mrs. T.

The day I came home, my mom and my sister are saying that I cannot be around my kids without supervision nor can I pick them up from school unless an authorized adult accompanies me, they can't spend the night with me under no circumstances. I am no longer living my life as a born again Christian, and it's high time to kick it into third gear with my relationship with God. If I do not, then prepare for total destruction. No, not on my watch. I called the CPS caseworker and had it explained to me but still just could not believe it. Lord, please help me! I cannot do this on my own.

I am not working, my dad has cancer, I am taking care of him, going to my meetings, going to counseling, taking anger management as a requirement of probation, I am taking the parenting classes, oh yea, no car, I wrecked it the night of the assault. I am back in church trying to regain Gods trust and favor. I am trying to rebuild my relationship with my kids. I have failed them as their mother. I'm dealing with so many emotions. Then my dad's condition is worsening. Even through all that; I still dealing with everything life's un-expectancies had in store for me. My dad slept away in Hospice at the Hospital the night of Feb 7 2013.

I'm so glad God has been the forefront and the foundation of our household, ever since I can remember. I love how He has to let things happen to us so that He is given all praise through our trials and tribulations. While in jail my granny sent a message to me to read the book of Job. I read every night before I went to bed. I have not nearly loss as much as Job, everything that happened going to jail and losing custody of my kids was God's plan to get me ready for what He has in store for me next. In April 2013 I regained custody of my kids not even one whole year were they from underneath my custody. God kept me! Thank you Lord! I was bitter, I snapped and jumped down throats at every turn, I defied the judicial system, I stayed in constant battle with my family and still; God kept me! I am indeed phenomenal; my future is bright; I can live that expected life! That is Phenomenal!

CHAPTER 12

MAKING PROGRESS, NOT EXCUSES

Kamekio Lewis

"A successful woman is one who can build a firm foundation with the bricks others have thrown at her."

IF I WAS a light skinned chic, maybe he would like me; is what I thought to myself as I stared at my reflection. I had been in the mirror for twenty minutes now, spraying spritz and working the bobby pins. "Mirror, Mirror on the wall who is"…never mind. If I had long hair, maybe she would be my friend and maybe I could eat lunch at the table with her and her crew, I just never knew. I never knew what it was like to be accepted and appreciated. If I were light skinned, with long hair, maybe, just maybe everything would be better. As I looked in the mirror, I saw a dark skinned, unhappy, little girl with plenty of problems. I realized that the reflection in my mirror made me sad. I was disappointed, because I wanted to be like her. I was frustrated because it seemed like she didn't have to try so hard to be pretty and accepted. Since I am ME, who I will always be, I worked with what I had; I embrace who I was and realized, she is me and I am her.

It was in that moment that I realized that I looked to people for validation. I continuously searched for a glimpse of confirmation; if they said it, it was my truth. I felt that I wasn't pretty enough…I just wasn't good enough. I looked at my nose, my eyes, and my hair. I sat there trying to figure out what could be fixed. I wanted people to like me, but as I stared in the mirror, I realized that I didn't even like me. In this skin, I felt stuck and limited to the opportunity of ever being happy. My mind was bombarded with thoughts of rejection and intimidation. I wanted the popularity, I wanted the glitz and the glamour, but it all seemed out of my reach. All these thoughts haunted me and because I thought these things, I became these things. I became depressed, full of self-pity, and vulnerable. I continued to look. I looked up and down; I even turned around, trying to see. I wanted to see beyond the skin and look deep within. I heard mamma when she said that, I heard her because she kept saying it, but I just couldn't see that pretty black girl. Yes, my mamma always said I was pretty, but she was mamma and she was supposed to say that. My mamma encouraged me and she believed in me, but I guess that just was not enough or was it?

We live in a world where too many girls are insecure about their looks. As I foolishly compared myself to other people, I felt less and less, I felt myself drifting lower and lower. If I had her hair, her skin, or her friends, maybe I would… It took me a long time to learn to just be me! I am black and I am beautiful! I realized it did not matter what other people were doing, it mattered what I was doing and sometimes it looked like I was doing absolutely nothing and going absolutely nowhere. I started with the reflection in the mirror and I was determined to change my ways. In my life, I dealt with a lot of doubt, insecurities and daddy issues, which I believe were directly related to my abusive relationship. As crazy as this seems, this is my truth. I share this with you because these are the things that I had to unpack and uncover in order to move on and live a life of peace and joy. I realized that there is so much purpose in my pain. I embrace me, I love me, I am black and I am beautiful. I have learned that it is not "If" I finish this or "If" I do that, it is when I finish this and when I do that.

The truth of the matter is I did what I knew to do. Before I enlisted in the United States Army, I had to take the ASVAB (Armed Service Vocational Aptitude Battery), which is a multiple-choice test, administered by MEPS (Military Entrance Processing Command) this test is used to determine qualifications for enlistment. I am sure you could never guess what job I qualified for? According to my ASVAB score my MOS (Military Occupation Specialty), would be MP (Military Police)! I remember the recruiter telling me that I was going to be an MP. At first I was confused, because I didn't know what MP meant and of course I asked, what is an MP? MP is the Military Police. I felt a hot chill go down my back and I got an instant headache. All I knew is that I could never go back to my hood and say that I was the police. Growing up, I was told that the police was the enemy. Growing up, I only had bad memories of the police and I did not want any part of that. I remember telling the recruiter, respectfully, no sir, I can't be the police! How ignorant was I? The truth of the matter is I did what I knew to do. Nobody ever told me that the police were good people and that they are here to protect & serve. Nobody ever said being a police officer is a real job with real benefits. As I did my research, I see that Police officers make good money, with the average salary of $47,996 per year. As awkward as it sounds, words like salary, 401K, and retirement were not part of our conversations.

In my hood, we didn't like the police! Seriously, Five-O was the enemy and when they came through we all ran. I remember as a little girl, being in the backyard building hay houses. Now, don't y'all act like y'all don't remember hay houses? Yes, I still remember, gathering all the hay in one pile, so I could get ready to build. My best friend and I would always compete to see who could build the biggest house and of course I always won. See, those were the days when little girls played in the backyard all day long, letting their imaginations run wild and having a good time. As I was contently playing and almost finished with my 3-bedroom house, I heard Lazy Larry holler Five–O and other people start echoing him and we all scattered like roaches. For a nine-year-old girl, this was traumatizing because I was really scared. I was scared because the police took people to jail and you didn't get to see them again for a long time. The police took your brothers and cousins away from you. I saw this over and over throughout my childhood, the police taking daddy out the home and leaving mamma back home, struggling! I remember running as fast as I could towards the house, I ran up in the house, tripping over my own feet, and breaking the hook off my red and white sandals. As I fell through mamma's front screen door, she start yelling at me, asking me why in the world was I making all that noise and slamming her door! Out of breath and heart beating 77 mph, I told her Five-O was outside. Mamma nosily ran to the door with her yellow and red housecoat on. She stood in the door, with the screen door wide open. I stood behind her, holding on to her leg, trying to see what was going on. My brother and sisters ran up in the house and started peeking through the blinds in the hallway and they know how mamma hated folk messing with her blinds. She turned around and started fussing at them, so they came down and stood behind me.

I was still scared and my heart was beating real fast, but I knew mamma would protect us! The people and the police were so loud! I was fixated on the noise, the lights, and the black and white cars. The police were everywhere and my eyes had never seen so many blue lights before. There looked as if there were one hundred police cars, surrounding one apartment! There were only about five, but to a nine-year-old girl, it was all the same! We watched as the police, slammed two of the boys on the ground and handcuffed them. The boys were scuffling like wild animals, like they were trying to get out. I kept trying to see who it was, but it was so many people outside, I could barely see. Mamma kept pushing me back up in the house, but I was trying so hard to see, I was so shocked to see it was Marcus and John John.

Ms. Mattie, their mom was cussing and screaming so loud that my mamma made me go back in the house. I hurried up and ran upstairs, so I could see. I looked out my bedroom window and just as I opened the curtain, I saw the police putting handcuffs on Ms. Mattie. I started screaming, "No, don't take Ms. Mattie"! Ms. Mattie was mamma's best friend and she kept us while mamma went to work. Who was gone keep us now? When I went back downstairs, I could hear mamma on the phone. She was telling somebody, "Chile they done took Mattie and those boys to jail. I told Mattie them boys gone be the death of her."

Mamma didn't know I was listening, so I went back upstairs, nervous and crying. I guess I cried myself to sleep, because when I woke up it was dark outside. I woke up thinking about what was going to happen to Ms. Mattie's boys. I just knew that I did not want Marcus to go back to jail, he was Tyesha's daddy and we just had a barbeque for him! The week before, I remember walking to the corner store and his brother; John John was saying that he was planning to go to college, he was saying something about a football scholarship, but he had to get his grades up. I am not sure what's going to happen to him now.

In my hood, we were like family, sitting on the porch and walking back and forth to the store all day getting penny candy and a Nehi peach. In the days of Lincoln Center, we hung our clothes on the clothesline, made hay houses, had wiener roast and played on the playground for hours. And though we talked and played all day, we knew the golden rule, be in the house before the streetlights came on! I remember there were many days you had to fight to get on the bus, fight on the bus, and just might have somebody waiting on you to fight when you got off the bus, but we loved on each other in a way that was unexplainable. In our own little world, we ran in and out of the door of our neighbor's house, toting plates, drinks, and popsicles. We sat on the front porch all day long laughing, fussing, and exchanging made up stories. We borrowed eggs, bread, flour, sugar, and the Kool aid. We always had somebody looking out for us, even if it was Ms. Mattie peeking out her window, trying to see what she could see. I saw Ms. Mattie going in her house. She was walking real slow and had her head down, I heard people whispering and saying that they kept the boys. I remember being so mad at the police and feeling real sad. I heard them say Marcus got 10 years and John John had to go to a Boys Home upstate. I started praying real hard for Ms. Mattie, and I made a promise to myself that I would never ever go to jail!

I somehow managed to keep the promise that I made to myself so many years ago. I managed to stay out of jail, but lived a life of pure hell. My self-esteem was already diminished, my negative thinking, produced a lot of negative outcomes. In this perfect storm, I thought I had arrived, because I navigated my way through. I had gotten out the hood, went to college and somehow did a U Turn back to Marcus. My mind was distorted, I was in bondage and I saw this relationship as a way of escape. I was older now and I knew better, but it was if my mind was playing tricks on me and my flesh had betrayed me! I never knew love, so this illusion of love had me twisted. I continued to rationalize my devious attraction. I had seen these types of dudes all my life and I was ignorantly attracted to the fast money, the rims, the attention, and the hype of the street life. I felt stuck in a whirlwind, going round and round. I was excited, yet lonely in this familiar place of lust, lies, and questionable behaviors. As a little girl, I never imagined a life filled with fears and tears. I was use to fighting, but never did I imagine that I would have to fight the man who said he loved me.

Many times, women have been manipulated, abused, and misguided for so long, that they lose sight of their own dreams, desires, and goals! I know the importance of having the support of family and friends, who will pray for you and love on you in spite of your situational behaviors and temporary insanity! When I think of the goodness of Jesus and all He's done for me, my soul cries out hallelujah, I thank God for saving me. I celebrate you and pray for your strength during this journey. It may seem that you have faced a lot of setbacks, but know that it is just a set up for God to show up and as you get up, rise boldly and walk in your authority.

In 1999, I was getting ready to graduate college, but I was lost, lonely, and confused. I had to push myself past the pain. I was in a twisted relationship that was full of lust, lies, and deceit. Not sure of my next move, I re-evaluated my current situation. I somehow expected the harvest to be different from the seeds I had planted. I had found Mr. Wrong, but it felt so right. I got caught up in his slick conversation, his manipulation, and the dollar signs. I was no longer on the outside looking in, but I was living in so much sin. I got caught up in a world of diamonds and disappointments. You see, the gifts were good, so his control felt like compassion through the eyes of daddy's little girl. The lust of the flesh felt like love everlasting, my dreams of feeling pretty, being loved, and being accepted had finally come true. I waited for a long time for a man to say to me "I love you!" I waited for a long time for a man to tell me "you are beautiful" and his backdoor approach catered to my unresolved issues and filled that space of loneliness and doubt. I thought he was helping me, but he was actually hindering me.

I was a little country girl, trying to make it on my own in this big old sinful world, stuck in the game, searching for fortune and fame. I admit, my dude was the dope boy and I ignorantly equated that to success. In my hood, to ride through bumping, with some rims, meant you were on. I was now the one behind the wheel, riding on some rims and bumping! As a little girl, I remember the excitement of seeing a car with rims come through and how mamma threatened to whoop me for running out the door trying to see. I knew this lifestyle was off limits for me and mamma told me a thousand times what not to do and who not to talk to, but I was just caught up in the hype! There was so much conversation about the dudes with the money, dudes who just got out, and the upcoming barbeques! And though mamma worked to keep me from this lifestyle and I got many whooping for leaving out the yard, I tested the waters and almost drowned! I didn't directly participate in this lifestyle, but I happily reaped all the benefits of being the girlfriend, from the money to the fame, linked to abuse and the shame. I admit I had some daddy issues, so this was my way of coping with that. I struggled with understanding the role of a man in my life. I sought attention and just wanted to be recognized, loved, and appreciated by a man. Marcus acknowledged me and made my presence known, so I subconsciously appreciated any time and attention that he gave me. I hid those awkward and uncomfortable feelings, with an expectancy to fail and go astray. I didn't understand then, what I was giving my attention to was shaping my mind and my character. I had gotten comfortable with kicking it, spending it, and risking it. It took me a long time, but I have learned to own that. I had lost sight of what was important. I was a mess wrapped up in my flesh!

It is only by the grace of God that I never got arrested or went to jail. In those days, I didn't understand the truth behind the devils plot of coming to kill, steal, and destroy; the enemy was trying to kill my dreams, steal my peace, and destroy my life. And he almost had me because I somehow stayed too long in a relationship that I knew had gone wrong. I foolishly let "I love him," distract me from "I love me!" I had to realize that this was just a distraction and a detour from my divine destiny and it was the only thing standing between me and my college degree. I always understood the importance of prayer, so daily I asked the Lord to help me to stay focused on my assignments and resist the temptation of the enemy!

As I began to grow through some things, I realized that this was not the end, but it was my beginning. It took a lot of strength, prayer and self-talks, but I was okay with that because I had a desire to be better. In my quest to love me and my desire to be better, I had to purposely plan. There was a grieving period and some lonely nights, but I stayed committed to me and focused on my purpose and not my pain. It was a stressful transition, but I took comfort in knowing that if things were going to change, I had to make some moves. I admit that I had gotten lost in materialistic things and consequently got off course. As I anchored myself in this reality, I couldn't see how this was going to work. I had been so damaged and disrespected and I couldn't wait on external things to change before I started to make some internal moves. My situation didn't change, my man didn't change, but my mind did. I had made up my mind that I was frustrated and irritated. In this place of frustration, I prayed and prayed and prayed. It was only by God's grace that I was able to endure. I was in some dangerous places and unforeseen troubles, but His grace brought me out, kept me, protected me, healed me, and delivered me from some evil ways, evil thinking, and evil doings. I believed everything that this dude said to me or at least I had to make him think that. His words had become my truth and his perception had become my reality.

Have you ever heard someone say, sticks and stones might break my bones, but words will never hurt me? Not true, words do hurt! Nobody wants to be teased and or talked about. As little girls, we want to fit in, be pretty, and have lots of friends. It is important for parents to teach and train their children and it helps when daddy encourages her and loves on her. Mothers, we play a very significant role, but for daddy to tell her that she is loved and appreciated and for him to continuously tell her she is beautiful is a beautiful and life changing thing. We must teach her to value her body and her mind. So, when Mister comes along, she is not caught up in his slick conversation and manipulation. Why? Because, mamma taught me to be a woman of noble character; who is worth far more than rubies, and who is clothed with strength and dignity. Why?

Because daddy has always told me that he loves me and he taught me to love me. Daddy taught me to trust in the Lord with all my heart and lean not to my own understanding and though sometimes I might not understand, I still know that God's grace is sufficient for me and that all things will work together for my good.

I no longer think about what my daddy didn't do or worry about what my daddy should've done. It took me a long time and though my daddy has gone on, I have learned to love, forgive, and let go. God has set me free from those past hurts and pains and I am no longer entangled in regrets and disappointments. I walk in my healing and deliverance and there is so much peace in this place!

It took me a long time to learn to dance in the rain. I learned to embrace ME and to appreciate the woman that I have become. I was determined to live beyond my past and no longer struggle and fight with yesterday's little girl! Yes, I have been through so much, but I have accomplished much more. Look at me now, a little black girl, from the projects, with a high school diploma, two college degrees, and a real good man. Actually, I never wanted to love again, because love hurt, but God! I am happily married, with three extremely handsome young men.

This is my truth and I will not allow anyone to condemn me or minimize my accomplishments. I decree and declare I am beautiful, I am powerful, and I am fearfully and wonderfully made! I've heard people say what does not kill you makes you stronger. I have learned that what did not kill me made me...ME. With the support and love from my children and my husband, I have learned to adore the beautiful woman in the mirror, encourage her, and pat her on the back. I love me; I love me from deep within, in my skin, wrapped up in my thoughts, visions and aspirations. I strive for better, not perfect, but I strive to operate in a spirit of excellence and integrity.

I am a survivor of domestic violence, and I too stayed when I knew I should have left. I too made excuses, hoping my abuser would change. I wanted to be loved and I wanted my relationship to work but by the grace of God, I am still here. If I had somewhere to go, maybe I would have left earlier? If I had a support system, maybe I could have, maybe I should have, but I didn't, because I was too embarrassed!

I know about domestic violence, because I was in a domestic violence relationship, but I was in it and I got out of it. Until recently, I blamed dude. I blamed him for all the bad things that happened to me, but I now take full responsibility for the role I played. I never knew that there were so many issues I had to deal with within myself.

On today, we take comfort in knowing that we are a phenomenal! God created us woman, we bring forth life, we push and give birth not only to babies, but to ideas and businesses. Yes, we are women and we create, transform, and nurture. We *Share Life* and we strive to capture the essence of every girl's dream, which is to be happy, healthy, and prosperous. We pledge to share our time, talents, and resources to help women, mentally, physically, spiritually, and financially. I have heard people say that prayer changes things; however I honestly believe that prayer changes people and it is up to us to change the things. I prayed for strength for this journey. It seemed like I had a lot of setbacks, but as I look back, I see that it was just a setup, for me to get up. I had to get up and make some moves, I had to get up and start pressing my way. I started to read my Bible more, I started going to church, and praying. I was grounded in that Word and I renewed my mind daily. It was hard because I had to learn to deny that flesh and those fleshy desires. I learned that I still had to fight, but now I understood that I was not fighting against flesh and blood, but this was a spiritual warfare. I am a soldier and I was ready for battle. I had to be fully prepped and prepared, because every day I was entering a warzone. There was nothing fun about my transition, but I stood firm and I knew that I could not be intimidated by the schemes of the devil and I continue to be bold and blessed in the things of God.

ABOUT THE AUTHORS

TRA-C J PIERCE
CEO/Author/Motivational Speaker/Entrepreneur

Tra-C J.Pierce is a multi-gifted and multi-dimensional woman with expertise in Education and Spanish. Originally from Houston, Texas, she has now found her life to be productive in Dallas-Fort Worth, where she studied at the University of Texas at Arlington. Tra-C realized at a young age that there was a call to the ministry upon her life, and because of this realization, she has begun to expand upon the things of God through writing, speaking, and conducting seminars. She is an author, motivational speaker, and entrepreneur. She has devoted her life to inspiring people world-wide with her messages of hope, health, and prosperity. Tra-C the writer and speaker is able to carefully articulate principals, standards, and concepts that the audience and readers are able to readily make applicable to their everyday life. Because of her excellence, she is able to effectively reach every generation as they turn the pages of her books and actively participate in her seminars. Her audiences are able to gain information and knowledge that will transform their way of thinking and increase the mentality levels of all who would dare to desire change. She is the founder of Phenomenal Women, an organization that helps women from all walks of life realize their potential and get to the next dimension. Tra-C has received multiple blessings in the areas of evangelism, exhortation, teaching, and worship. Because evangelism is the initial stage for transforming lives, she has confidently enlisted her time and energy toward those who will listen. Her desire is to convey the very heartbeat and pulse of true purpose while removing a false hope that renders many individuals helpless. Through evangelism and living an evangelistic life, of which she is an example, Tra-C's presence alone renders exhortation and a strong urge that destroys bondage. Her overall mission is to release captives free and escort prisoners of poverty into the Kingdom of prosperity. Tra-C understands that with what God has assigned her to do she must be disciplined, which requires great sacrifice, obedience, consecration, cleanliness, and holiness. She has dedicated her life first to God, to her family, and to ministry. She is a wife of twenty-two years, and a mother of two children, who have received firsthand the life-changing experiences that Tra-C has to offer to the nation

www.phenomenalwo-man.com

https://www.facebook.com/phe1234?fref=ts

Evangelist Patsy Cross-Cole, CBT

Conference Speaker/Evangelist /Mentor/Certified Belief Therapist/ Health & Wellness Coach

Founder & CEO – Be Made Whole Ministries

Live…Love…Laugh is not just her motto; Patsy emulates this on a daily basis. As a blessed wife and mother of 5, she intentionally embraces each God-given day by displaying charity and expressing joy to all those she encounters. It has always been her heart's desire to help people and to make a difference in the lives of others. As an advocate for the disadvantaged, she realized that all people are important and everyone has the potential for greatness.

Although Patsy received salvation at a young age, she discovered the intentions of God for her life in 1998, and accepted the ministry call to *"Do the work of an Evangelist"*. Due to her hidden, yet, traumatic past of childhood molestation, FEAR continued the attempt to sabotage her destiny. However, in 2011, Patsy defeated the odds and became the *Founder of Be Made Whole Ministries*, which focuses on holistic healing of the *spirit, soul and body*. Its mere existence is to *empower, encourage* and *equip* others to move beyond their painful past and present challenges into a purpose-driven life. As a survivor of divorce, single parenthood, and health challenges (Fibromyalgia) and molestation, Patsy understands what it means to overcome challenges prevalent in today's society. She longs to see others transformed from feelings of inadequacy and insignificance to lives of confidence and influence.

A sought after conference speaker, Patsy takes the hope and healing message to religious and secular events. Her passionate delivery and transparent heart, captivates and delights audiences of all ages, genders and backgrounds. Each message is rich with Scripture, real life stories, candor, practical steps and relevant analogies. Her presentations shine with clarity and engaging examples while stirring the heart of those who seek emotional and spiritual freedom. Patsy has a published article entitled "*Sharing My Story*" in

Run On Magazine and has appeared as a guest on *Joshua Generation Radio* and *Radio Therapy with Terance J.*

She holds fast to the truth that people are able to conquer any adversity they may face. As a Mentor, Patsy's compelling passion for women's ministry and to help hurting humanity is ever-increasing. She hosted *Meet Me in the Spirit* Women's Conference in 2007-2008 and *Reveal Your Glory Women's Gathering* in 2015. Patsy earned a Bachelor of Science degree and received her certification as a Belief Therapist in 2012 from Therapon Bible Institute. She is a member of Delta Sigma Theta Sorority and a recipient of Who's Who among Students in Colleges and Universities. As an aspiring author, Patsy endeavors to persuade her readers to discover the pathway to freedom and wholeness. She is currently working on her 3rd Book Project as a Co-Author. Patsy is also excited about the curriculum development and publication for her *Free to Be Free* Workshops launch in 2016!

Without a doubt, this earthen vessel has truly had an encounter with God. In result, He has released upon her a fresh prophetic and healing anointing. As God continues to build His character in her, Patsy is truly learning what it means to go from *faith to faith and from glory to glory.*

www.bmadewholeministries.org

Email: bmadewholecenter@yahoo.com

Facebook: Author Patsy Cross-Cole

Evangelist Patsy Cole

Mia Turner-Whitley

Wife/ Mother/ Grandmother/ Facilitator and Learning Consultant/ Author

Mia Turner-Whitley is co-author of "No Glory without a Story". It is a book about various life struggles from a group of victorious overcomers. Mia's story is about how God healed her broken heart after a terrible divorce. She talks about the highs and lows of going through a divorce while both parties are in church and working within the ministry. It was a very trying time, but God has healed her, matured her and blessed her to marry her King. Mia is an active member of a Dallas non-profit organization called ANTHEM strong families. She is one of the Lead Facilitators. Her specialty includes engaged and married couples workshops, as well as workshops for families. Mia loves the opportunity to uplift, encourage and empower others in their relationships. She won the coveted 2012 Facilitator of the year from ANTHEM and continues to provide excellent workshops. Mia is also an active member of her sorority Zeta Phi Beta, Incorporated. She is one of the facilitators for the Stork's Nest Program. This program is partnered with March of Dimes and provides workshops on educating underprivileged expecting parents on having a healthy pregnancy and childbirth. Mia is a newlywed married to Mr. Pedro Whitley. They have a blended family of 7 (6 young adults and one teenager) children and 11 grandchildren. She strongly believes in the family as the core unit of society. Mia has over 17 years of customer service experience as a Learning Consultant/Facilitator. She has earned a Bachelor's in Psychology and Education. She has earned two Masters. Mia's first Masters is in Human Resource Management and her second Master's is in Organizational Instructional development. Her dream is to become an International Motivational Speaker and Writer.

miaspeaks@gmail.com

Joyce Petry Montgomery

Mother/Faith Counselor/Truly Virtuous Ministry Mentor/Author

Joyce M. Montgomery is a native of Oberlin Louisiana; she is the seventh of eight children Joyce graduated for Skyline High School, Dallas,

Texas. Joyce also attended Central Texas Commercial College. Joyce is the wife of Corey Montgomery and they have been married for three years. Joyce is the mother of two beautiful children, Joshua and Joycelyn Taylor. Joyce also has a blended family she is step mother to Chasidy, Corey, Jr. and Courtney Montgomery.

Joyce is a dedicated member of The Union Church of Dallas, Texas. She is a faithful member of the Voices of Judah Choir, she participates in the hospitality ministry, and she is a Faith Counselor and the Women's ministry. Joyce is a four year Cancer Survivor. Joyce is the leader of the CARE Ministry. Joyce mentors ladies and gentlemen that have or had cancer. She has been working in the Mortgage Industry for over fifteen years. Joyce is dedicated to reaching and touching the lives of people she comes in contact with, whether she can help them or offer a smile or a kind word. Life Matters to Joyce!

https://www.facebook.com/joyce.p.montgomery?fref=ts

Dr. Sarah Ransom

Dr/Prophetess/Author/Mother-Grandmother/Conference Speaker

Dr. Sarah Ransom is the founder and CEO of Ransom's Creations Ministries, an international ministry that was founded to equip and encourage people to come into their heavenly designed purpose, to be ambassadors of the Kingdom and affect their sphere of influence for the Kingdom of God. Dr. Ransom believes in education and has been blessed to receive an honorary Doctorate in Divinity from WCM (World Christianship Ministries) in Fresno, CA and has earned a Masters and Bachelors in Theological Studies from Vision International University, Ramona, CA and will soon complete her Ph. D. degree.

Dr. Ransom was born to the lovely parents of William Ransom (deceased) and Margaret Ransom in Milford, Texas USA, on August 29, 1965. She is the 5th child of eight children.

Dr. Sarah ministers throughout the U.S. and soon to take on internationally, and across denominational boundaries, with a vibrant prophetic teaching ministry as well as a healthy understanding of the Office of a Prophet – that brings order to the government of the church.

Dr. Ransom is a federal government contractor for SBA (Small Business Administration) Disaster Assistance Program. Dr. Sarah has been with SBA as Sr. Loan Officer and Legal Assistant, since inception date of September 26, 2005, serving thousands of misplaced victims during Hurricane Katrina. Dr. Ransom has worked for other companies and organizations such as: American Cancer Society, Dillard's Corporate Buying Office, Tom James Company-Retailer, Walmart Stores, Cigna Healthcare, Blue Cross Blue Shield, Texas Insurance group, St. Paul Insurance Companies, Travelers Insurance, Corliss Stones-Littles, Inc., Stephen Pierce International, Inc., and Bank of America Corporation.

Dr. Ransom is a ordain minister under the tutelage of Dr. Renee Hornbuckle, Our Agape Church-Arlington, Texas. Dr. Ransom is a recent divorcee and a proud mother of three wonderful children and one granddaughter. She resides in Grand Prairie, Texas (Joe Pool area) with youngest son and daughter.

https://www.facebook.com/saraharansom?fref=t

Kendra Dee

Motivational Speaker/Writer/International Missionary Mentor/Author

Kendra Dee is a powerful motivational speaker/writer, international missionary, mentor, and rising author. For the past several years, Kendra has devoted her time towards advocacy and heightening awareness for the plights of the orphaned, abused, abandoned and oppressed in West Africa, with primary focus on the people of Nigeria and Ghana. She also volunteers her time as a tutor and advisor to disadvantaged or academically-challenged kids and teens. Kendra is a native of the northeastern US, but was raised in Texas, which she and her family proudly call home.

https://www.facebook.com/misskd1972?fref=ts

Dianne "Pastor di" Matthews

Teacher/Social Scientist/Writer/Orator/Life Coach

Dianne Matthews, affectionately known as Pastor di, is a native of Dallas, Texas. She is a mother of 2, grandmother of seven. Pastor di is a breast cancer survivor approaching the 4 year mark.

Pastor di, was an early graduate of Skyline High School class of 1976. She enrolled in Texas Southern University, Houston, Texas in the school of Public Affairs stayed one year and decided to attend the University of Houston as a Political Science major where she stay until 1979. Bored with college because she spent more time on the road with her church and Pastor doing crusades across the United States; she dropped out of college for a moment to determine what she really wanted to do. After a semester of contemplation she enrolled in Bishop College in 1979-80, as a Christian Education major. Bishop helped her gain a perspective and she left Bishop and returned to Houston Texas.

It took several years of moving from Dallas to Houston and back to Dallas before Pastor di found herself and her calling. In 1991 she enrolled in the Mt Zion Bible College Houston Texas where she stayed until she received a Doctorate in Theology. In September of 1992, she preached her initial sermon confirming her calling as a Gospel Minister; she was licensed and ordained at that time due to the extensive time in ministry. After completion of her Doctorate, she returned to Dallas to be among family and continue in ministry. In 2001 she founded The Philadelphia Church Ministries where she was Pastor for several years until health issues became overwhelming. As she conquered health issues she saw new opportunities in ministry. Ministering to the whole man became her focus and she began preparing to do so by enrolling in Kaplan University in 2008. Pastor di received her Bachelor's of Science in Health and Wellness in November 2011 while in the middle of Chemotherapy for the Breast Cancer. Pastor di enrolled in Capella University December of 2011 received a Master's of Science in Human Behavior Studies in June of 2013. Pastor di began a PhD program at Capella in 2013 and expects to be complete by the end of 2015.

Pastor di received two Honorary Doctorates in 2010. She is Pastor, Preacher, Writer, Editor, Social Scientist, Motivational Speaker, Cook Extraordinaire, not a chef but a self taught cook. She enjoys being in the kitchen as much as she does the pulpit. She is a critical thinker and a lover of humanity. Pastor di considers herself as just a humble servant that was called to the people to lift them up to reach the place they were destined to go; just one of the least in the Kingdom with Great responsibility.

dimat40@yahoo.com

Teresa Beene

Wife/ Mother/ Volunteer and Leader of Children's Ministry

Teresa Beene is a 39 year old woman with 4 wonderful men in her life. Teresa is wife to her husband of 17 years; a mother to 2 sons, and her stepson whom she adores. Teresa has lived in Texas for the last 18 years. Teresa is a military veteran. Teresa works as a site manager and a financial coordinator for a medical office. Teresa is a dedicated member of Union Church and serves as a leader in the children's ministry. Teresa's favorite past time is spending time with her family.

https://www.facebook.com/teresa.beene?fref=ts

Jennifer Nash

Mentor/ Minister/Homeless Advocate/ Caterer /Mommy

Jennifer Nash, a single mother of 4, was born and raised in Chicago, Illinois. She has over 7 years of experience working as a Head Start Teacher. She has over 15 years working in ministry; working with women and children. Her passion is working with Homeless families and cooking. She has been volunteering on and off with different homeless ministries for over 9 years. Jennifer partnered with a friend in a catering business when she lived in Chicago. She currently working towards her own nonprofit homeless ministry for women called "Women of Divine Virtue Restoration Ministries." In her spare time she's doing other hobbies that she's gifted in and volunteering with other ministries. Jennifer currently resides in Dallas, Texas with her children. She is working towards her Culinary Degree so that she can start a new catering business, while maintaining her homeless ministry.

https://www.facebook.com/jennifer.nash.376?fref=ts

Kayla Roberts

Evangelist /Mentor/Account Manager Kayla Roberts is a 45 year old woman born in Shreveport Louisiana, raised in Longview, Texas. She graduated from Longview High School in 1988. Kayla also graduated from Texas State Technical College in 2005 with an AAS degree in Software Engineering: a minor in Professional Office Technology. Kayla moved to the Dallas Forth Worth area in 2010 from Monroe Louisiana. She presently works for Air General Inc at DFW Airport where she is an Account Manager for Lufthansa Cargo and Qantas Airline. Kayla is looking to God to see where he wants her to be as far as her career is concerned.

Kayla was ordained in ministry as an Evangelist in 1998 in Longview, Texas. Kayla currently worships at Bondage Breaking Ministries in Lancaster, Texas. She has 1 beautiful daughter and 3 handsome sons. She has 2 granddaughters and 2 grandsons. She is currently divorced and a stroke survivor. Kayla's passion is ministering to young woman who are at risk of or struggling through Teen pregnancies, Domestic Violence and Self esteem issues, her goal is to lead them out of those places as God lead her out, Through mentoring, teaching and sharing she encourages these women. She also shares with men by uplifting and encouraging them to be the Kings God has called them to

https://www.facebook.com/kayla.r.sauls?fref=ts

Alida Smith

Daughter/Sister/Mother/Business Administrator

Born the afternoon of February 11, 1978 in Wichita, KS; Alida is a woman of grace and laughter. Looking at her you would not believe she is the proud mother of six beautiful children. With warmth and love in her heart she is not one that meets a stranger. Her personality exudes her radiant and bubbly features. Once you get to know Alida, it is easy to understand how she does what she does and with pleasure. Alida is a person that loves to love and will go out of her way to lend a helping hand. She is optimistic and will seek out the good in any situation. Alida is a member of Freedom Missionary Baptist Church in Dallas, TX. She is an active member of the women's ministry in the church. Alida is no stranger to the workforce. Having been employed since the age of 16 through various positions, she has been in the field of skip-tracing for over 10 years. Alida enjoys making time for her other entrepreneurial adventures to help with the support of her family. Alida also is a Charter member and Business Coordinator for the Phenomenal Woman Organization founded by Tra-C J. Pierce. Her hobbies and special likes include spending time with family, playing volleyball, listening to music, dancing, fancy dining and shopping.

https://www.facebook.com/alida.smith.520?fref=ts

Kamekio Lewis

Author/ Playwright/Domestic Violence

Advocate/Speaker / Trainer

Serving others with Passion, Perseverance and Poise.

Surviving a 2 year abusive relationship fueled her passion to help other women in similar situations and motivated her to write her 1st book, "Looking for Love....In All the Wrong Places. The community support was overwhelming and she used the book as the basis to continue to bring awareness to domestic violence and wrote and produced her first Hit Stage Play in 2012 to a sold out crowd in Memphis, TN. Her mission is to continue to use print, publications, and plays to help bring awareness to the seriousness of domestic violence.

She found love in the right place and has been married to the love of her life, Dennis for 14 years. They have 3 handsome boys, Kaveyon, Kemareyon & Dakaree!

Kamekio has a passion to share the love of God through ministry and fellowship with women and children. She has continuously worked in the helping field throughout her military career in Alaska, Kansas, and now in Tennessee. She completed her Masters in Vocational Rehabilitation Counseling and has worked 10 years in the rehabilitation field, helping individuals with disabilities transition from school to work. Her passion to help others succeed is demonstrated through her countless volunteer hours and outreach ministries. She is the Executive Director of A New Day Rehabilitation & Counseling Services, a nonprofit organization whose mission is to eliminate transitional barriers and coordinate services for women and children to help them safely and successfully transition into education & employment.

An author, facilitator, and public speaker, Kamekio provides transitional coaching and consulting to equip and empower individuals with the skills, confidence, and resources, needed to safely & successfully transition. She shares her story of helplessness and hopelessness to show women that they are not alone! Her testimony has informed, inspired, and encouraged women to hope, stand on faith, and walk in love, as they transition from being the victim to being victorious!

ACHIEVEMENTS& AWARDS:

- 2009 Graduate of Ministry Training International
- 2011 Alpha Kappa Alpha Vanessa R Long Humanitarian Award
- 2012 Heal the Hood Game Changer Humanitarian & Advocacy Award
- 2012 Finalist for Memphis Best in Black Awards

- Member of "The National Coalition of 100 Black Women"
- Member of Tennessee Coalition to End Domestic Violence
- Member of National Rehabilitation Association
- Member of Alpha Kappa Alpha (Phi Lambda Omega Chapter)
- 8 Years United States Army
- Currently Pursuing Doctoral Degree

Please visit: www.kamekiolewis.com

Made in the USA
Middletown, DE
18 May 2020